TWAYNE'S WORLD AUTHORS SERIES

A Survey of the World's Literature

Sylvia E. Bowman, Indiana University

GENERAL EDITOR

DENMARK

Leif Sjöberg, State University of New York
at Stony Brook

EDITOR

Johannes Jörgensen

(*TWAS* 70)

TWAYNE'S WORLD AUTHORS SERIES (TWAS)

The purpose of TWAS is to survey the major writers —novelists, dramatists, historians, poets, philosophers, and critics—of the nations of the world. Among the national literatures covered are those of Australia, Canada, China, Eastern Europe, France, Germany, Greece, India, Italy, Japan, Latin America, New Zealand, Poland, Russia, Scandinavia, Spain, and the African nations, as well as Hebrew, Yiddish, and Latin Classical literatures. This survey is complemented by Twayne's United States Authors Series and English Authors Series.

The intent of each volume in these series is to present a critical-analytical study of the works of the writer; to include biographical and historical material that may be necessary for understanding, appreciation, and critical appraisal of the writer; and to present all material in clear, concise English—but not to vitiate the scholarly content of the work by doing so.

Johannes Jörgensen

By W. GLYN JONES

University College, London

Twayne Publishers, Inc.　::　New York

Foreword

THE AIM of this book is to demonstrate the essential unity of Johannes Jörgensen's work and to show how he uses his books as vehicles for his own self-expression, however far removed from him some of the themes appear to be. To do this, it has seemed to me reasonable to break with a strictly chronological arrangement, and instead to treat Jörgensen's books according to the various categories to which they belong.

Likewise, in a book which will be read by an audience many of whom do not understand Danish, it has seemed natural to me to avoid any detailed stylistic discussion and to concentrate instead on the development of ideas within Jörgensen's work. I have accordingly contented myself with relatively brief indications of style where I considered these relevant.

Although much of Jörgensen's work is available in English translation, I have chosen to make my own translations of all the quoted matter so as to achieve uniformity and also in order to come as close as possible to a literal translation of the Danish. When quoting from Jörgensen's prose I have not thought it necessary to furnish the Danish text, but I have included the original lines in the case of some of the poetry.

My thanks are due to the Gyldendal publishing house of Copenhagen for permission to quote from Jörgensen's work.

Where fitting, I have used material from my own earlier book on Jörgensen, *Johannes Jörgensens modne år*, and the chapter on Jörgensen's novels contains material from an article I wrote on this subject in *Scandinavian Studies* in 1964.

I would like to express my sincere thanks to my friend and colleague Anthony Petti of the Department of English in University College for an extremely careful reading of the manuscript and for the numerous suggestions he made for improvements in it.

My thanks are also due to the Rask-Örsted Fund, Copenhagen, for support in the preparation of this book.

W. G. J.

University College, London
Whitsun, 1968

Contents

Chronology

1866 Jörgensen born November 6 in Svendborg.
1882 Moved to Copenhagen.
1887 *Verse.*
1888 *Spring Legend.*
1891 First marriage.
1892 First meeting with Ballin.
1893 Editor of *Taarnet.*
1894 First journey abroad.
1895 *The Book of Travel.*
1896 Received into Catholic Church.
1898 Editor of *Katholiken.*
1900 *Our Lady of Denmark.*
1902 Second visit to Rome.
1903 *The Book of the Pilgrim.*
1907 *St. Francis of Assisi.*
1913 Separation from his wife.
1914 Meeting with Andrée Carof.
     Settled in Siena.
1915 Civil divorce.
     Moved to Assisi.
     St. Catherine of Siena.
1916– *The Legend of My Life*, I-VI.
1919
1921 Journey to Palestine.
1922 Citizen of honor of Assisi.
1927 Honorary Ph.D., Louvain.
1928 *The Legend of My Life*, VII.

1933   Death of Andrée Carof.
1934   *Charles de Foucauld.*
1936   Citizen of honor of Svendborg.
      Honorary Ph.D., Stockholm.
1937   Second marriage.
1939   Moved to Vadstena.
1941   Moved to Denmark.
      St. Bridget of Sweden, I.
1943   *St. Bridget of Sweden, II.*
1945   Awarded the Holberg Medal.
1946   Returned to Assisi.
1953   Returned to childhood home in Svendborg.
1956   Died May 29 in Svendborg.

CHAPTER 1

Background and Biography

I The Cultural Scene

THE 1860s were a period of vacuum in Danish cultural life. Of the great figures of the Romantic age only two were still alive—Hans Christian Andersen (d. 1875) and N. F. S. Grundtvig (d. 1872)—but as literary influences they had ceased to be of prime importance, and Grundtvig's theological ideas belonged to a limited circle only. The other outstanding Romantic, Adam Oehlenschläger, had died in 1850, while Sören Kierkegaard had died five years later. As these authors had either died or grown old, no one had emerged to replace them or to introduce viable new ideas. Meïr Aaron Goldschmidt, the editor of *The Corsair* (*Corsaren*) during its feud with Kierkegaard, was a popular novelist whose literary merits were recognized then as now, and who progressed some way along the path from Romanticism to Realism. His only companion was Hans Egede Schack, whose novel *The Phantasts* (*Phantasterne*, 1857) did represent a new departure, being an intense psychological study such as had not been seen before. Though it retains a considerable amount of Romantic trappings, this book is essentially a warning against Romantic daydreaming and a call to accept everyday reality even though the hero does finally marry a princess in the true Romantic fashion. Schack died young, having completed only this one novel, and it is difficult to claim that he represented a new literary departure; indeed, what is known of his fragmentary novel, *Truth with Modification* (*Sandhed med Modifikation*), scarcely fulfills the promise of *The Phantasts*.

This halting movement toward greater realism in literature would doubtless sooner or later have resulted in a new period of literary production. Meanwhile, the critic Georg Brandes (1842-1927) emerged, and in 1871 he gave a series of lectures on *Main Currents in Nineteenth Century European Literature,* a brilliant if somewhat onesided analysis of modern European thought, and in so doing he introduced into Denmark many of the new ideas which were sweeping through Europe at large in the second half of the nineteenth century. He introduced the critical methods of Sainte Beuve and Taine, the positivist philosophy of Auguste Comte, the philosophy of John Stuart Mill. He referred to the radical theological ideas of Strauss and Feuerbach, and to Darwin's theories on the evolution of man. Marxist ideas were also discussed, though Brandes did not stress them, and they played relatively little part in the immediate development of Danish thought. All this was new in a country whose literature, political concepts and, to some extent, religious ideas (thanks to Grundtvig) were insular. Following the campaign of 1849 Denmark had seen a period of unrealistic and romantically tinged patriotism which had expressed itself in all areas of public life and in all aspects of its culture, and this patriotism had persisted after Denmark's defeat by Prussia in 1864. Despite the disillusionment which this brought about, Denmark continued to be inward-looking and to ignore, or be ignorant of, ideas outside her own boundaries. These ideas would have penetrated even without Brandes—indeed Darwin had been translated in part before Brandes popularized him—but to Brandes has gone the credit for the upsurge of new and predominantly radical ideas in the 1870s and 1880s. He was responsible not merely for their literary expression, but also for the new radical movement in politics, based on idealistic humanism and social indignation; his influence permeated Danish cultural life in its entirety, and it is thanks to him that Danish literature since his day has been largely, though by no means exclusively, socialist and atheist in its sympathies.

The new generation of authors, mostly prose writers, were eager in one way or another to adopt Brandes' ideas and express them in their work. Ironically enough, the first of his followers, Jens Peter Jacobsen (1847-85), had been making his mark as a lyric poet before Brandes came on the scene, but though he continued to write experimental verse, he now concentrated on prose of lyrical quality. His novels show a greater psychological pre-occupation and insight than anything which had preceded him, and he tried to write on a purely Darwinian basis, showing Man to be part of nature, a creature of instinct; still, he did not seek to produce degrading or brutal portrayals, as did some minor Darwinian writers. Moreover, he aimed at photographic precision of expression, resorting to neologisms and home-made compounds to achieve this. Thus his prose became a vehicle of the new scientific approach to literature, combining lyricism and color with the observation of a botanist. Radical in the sense of having accepted the ideas Brandes had introduced into Denmark as a basis for his thought, Jacobsen was, however, not a man to engage in agitation.

One of his contemporaries, Holger Drachmann (1846-1908), also a lyric poet, was, however, such a man, and he used his poetry in order to make propaganda for the new ideals. He did not, however, remain true to his original Brandesian-socialist principles, but wavered between them and a more Romantic and conservative outlook. From his early energetic and powerful works in support of the Brandesian problem debate, he proceeded to more truly lyrical outbursts occasioned by his own problems rather than by the social debate in the world around him. In all these, however, and in his ballad-like character poems, he experimented with themes new to Danish poetry and with new forms of expression. In particular, he broke down what were the traditional verse forms of Danish Romanticism, the regular lines and verses which had been observed and elaborated on by poets for the past sixty years. He made use of enjambement and the irregular appearance of lines half the length of those on which the poem was based, or half as long again, thus producing a poetic expression which is indeed rhythmical, but in which the rhythm is varied at will, or in which it is on occasion completely abandoned for the direct inclusion of a prose exclamation. In this he was subsequently to be of considerable importance to Johannes Jörgensen, who in his first two verse collections proceeded to build on the foundations of verse technique laid by Drachmann, and to create for himself a new, infinitely supple verse form which at times approaches free verse. There is little to distinguish Jörgensen's freer verse from his prose poems, the ultimate inspiration for which is the lyrical prose of Jens Peter Jacobsen.

Despite their support of Brandesian literary ideals, Drachmann and Jacobsen were not typical of the new movement: their work was too colorful, their prose too lyrical for a later generation to see them as typical in their mode of expression, even if their general philosophical attitude was that of the Brandes movement. More typical was Sophus Schandorff, with his naturalistic novels of provincial life, while the outstanding novelist among them was Henrik Pontoppidan, whose early novels and short stories betray a preoccupation with social problems and the political situation of the day. He was concerned, in a critical manner, with the position of the church in Denmark, and with the importance which should be attached to the various religious movements in the country. His analysis of them shows them as consisting mainly of self-seeking and insufficiency, and even as late as 1917, in his last major novel, *The Realm of the Dead* (*De Dödes Rige*), he describes how a man who has undergone a true religious experience is hounded by the established church. In this attitude toward the church he was doubtless to some extent influenced by Kierkegaard's attack earlier in the century, but his general outlook was far removed from Kierkegaard and more closely related to that of Georg Brandes. The fourth outstanding figure of the "modern breakthrough," as the Brandesian movement came to be called, was Herman Bang, who moved from the grayness of naturalistic prose and social problems to an impressionistic portrayal of life in the provinces and the capital, in which his sympathy was with those who were ill used or overlooked by the prosperous and the indifferent. He was less outspoken in his opinions than Pontoppidan and most of the minor writers of the movement, but he shared their ideas on Darwinism and atheism.

This was the movement of the young. All accepted conventions and institutions were subjected to the attack of the younger writers, while on a different level politicians sought to put the ideas of the movement into practice. The younger intellectuals were almost to a man atheistic or anticlerical; marriage as an institution was questioned and ignored; in politics the young were left-wing and sought to make contact with the working classes and to find common ground with them in their opposition to the paternalistic moneyed classes. At the same time they questioned the effectiveness of this paternalist treatment of social inferiors, pointing out the abuse and the hardship which resulted from it. There was, as a result of the radical words of Brandes and his immediate followers, an awakening of the public conscience which found expression in every conceivable walk of life, in art, literature, society, indeed in theology itself with its new views inspired by Strauss and Auerbach.

These new ideas were actively and vociferously opposed by the older generation who rightly saw the entire foundation of the culture in which they had grown up being undermined. Intolerance grew on both sides, as always happens when new ideas fire the minds of a young generation, and the press was filled with spirited debates. Parents did their best to keep their children from establishing contact with liberal thought, and there are many accounts of homes in which the new literature was forbidden and newspapers of liberal inclination proscribed. It was all to little avail, and few of the intellectuals of the new generation were able to subscribe to the old standards.

Thus, for twenty years Danish thought and literature were dominated by radical ideas. Literature, apart from that of the few outstanding writers, became a vehicle for debate. Lyricism was almost completely excluded, and any thought of a transcendental reality was anathema. Even Drachmann in his more conservative moods made no allusion to this. The general feeling was that religion was unlikely to survive for more than a few years.

By the late 1880s the immediate sympathies of the young still lay with the radicals, but their thirst for something new in literature grew with the increasing awareness of the fact that the general run of literature consisted of varying degrees of grayness. Even as early as 1884 Karl Gjellerup (awarded the Nobel Prize jointly with Pontoppidan in 1917) had turned from the naturalistic ideal and the new moral standards which accompanied it, and was embarking on a course which took him far from subsequent Danish thought. This younger generation of writers looked for beauty for its own sake, and occupied themselves with poetic form in a manner which was completely foreign to the prose writers of the seventies and eighties. Verse was their medium, and they sought to find a new poetical expression, which emerged as something akin to the Symbolism which was being developed in France at the same time. The term "Symbolism" was in fact used by the new Danish poets in their program writings, and although they used it in various senses, it did indicate the revolt against the prosaic Naturalism of the preceding years and the attempt to produce by poetic means something which naturalistic description fails to achieve. The new writers were attracted by the conciseness of the French poetry—the main impulses coming from Baudelaire, Verlaine, and Mallarmé—and the way in which they made their effect through apparent simplicity of language and verse form. In addition, they were in varying degrees influenced by the Symbolists' idea of a transcendental reality, the notion that behind the façade of nature there was a deeper reality which it was their task to present to their readers and themselves. They were further inspired in this by Nietzsche, most especially by his "Midnight Song" from *Also Sprach Zarathustra:* "die Welt ist tief, und tiefer als der Tag gedacht." In his essay on J. K. Huysmans in the periodical *Tilskueren* (*The Spectator*) Jörgensen summed up his attitude to the old, materialistic view of life as follows:

The view above us is blocked for modern man. There is nothing to live for except the life we live day by day—and, in the opinion of the new orthodoxy, neither ought there to be any other. From now onwards man is enclosed in a completely material and finite world— and when death comes, then all is past. From this it follows that life is felt more and more to be something restricted, straightforward, trivial—something one can treat according to mood and desire. It is forgotten that life is a miracle, a mystery, a sacred thing, to be lived with awe. The modern lack of moral standards is a result of the modern lack of metaphysics.[1]

Jörgensen here stressed the metaphysical aspect of reality more than his contemporaries, although Sophus Claussen also wrote in similar tones on occasion. Nor was there as yet any thought of directly Christian metaphysics, though the step from an argument in favor of a generalized transcendental reality with its effect on moral standards to a specifically Christian view of life was not a great one. Furthermore, Jörgensen was always a moralist, and it was partly his failure to found a moral code on his vague, pantheistic metaphysics which brought him back to Christianity.

He was, however, the only one of the original poets of the 1890s to take this stand. Viggo Stuckenberg remained fixed in his metaphysically tinged cult of the ego, gazing deep into his own soul, but remaining a god unto himself, while Sophus Claussen was content to react against the grayness and neo-rationalism of the 1870s and 1880s and rejoice in life and beauty for their own sake. He remained less dogmatic in his conceptions than either Stuckenberg or Jörgensen, and he kept his contacts with both of them when their widely differing views of life led to an estrangement between them.

II *Jörgensen's Life*

Born in 1866 in the small town of Svendborg on the south coast of the island of Fyn, Johannes Jörgensen spent his formative years during the height of the Brandesian movement. His meeting with it was decisive for him in that it resulted in a twofold conflict within him. On the one hand, there was the conflict caused by the meeting between the provincial life he had known at home and the life he found in the capital city when he went there at the age of 16. On the other, there was the clash between the religious and moral upbringing of his childhood and the antireligious and amoral attitudes which he now encountered. To some extent these conflicts were different aspects of one and the same thing, but they were not identical.

He was the son of a sailor, and due to his father's long absences from home he appears to have been particularly susceptible to the influences of his mother and his uncle. From his mother he inherited a religious turn of mind; when he was a child she had left the Danish State Church and had become a Methodist, and he was brought up under the influence of Methodism, though he appears never to have been particularly receptive to it. The tenderness and uncomplicated faith he met in his mother were supplemented by a love of nature and a passion for literature which his mother's brother, Jörgen Johansen, inspired in him. In particular, uncle Jörgen introduced him to Goethe, Heine, and the whole of the German Romantic movement, impulses which were to be of supreme importance to him in later years.

He subsequently felt obliged to break with German Romanticism and the pantheism which is the basis of much of it, but even after his conversion, when he felt himself "based on reality" in Catholicism, he felt drawn to the Romantic poetry of Denmark's neighbor to the south; in *The Book of Travel* this urge to return to the Romantic poetry he had left is used to symbolize the fascination which his pre-Catholic life still held for him for a period.

There was no secondary school or any school on college level in Svendborg at that time, and a few months before his sixteenth birthday Jörgensen went to Copenhagen to continue his schooling—a mere year or so older than Hans Christian Andersen had been when he went from his birthplace to the capital. And like Andersen, Jörgensen had to undergo much suffering in his early years. He was scarcely as poor as Andersen had been, but he still had to live in very modest circumstances, and also underwent the difficulties experienced by many boys from the provinces on moving to the capital: a feeling of being different, of coming from a different cultural background. In addition, he felt himself to be ugly—he talks of his Mongol face—and to be completely out of place among his school friends. Indeed, he continually felt "different" from his countrymen throughout his life, and on one occasion surmised that he might have Spanish blood in his veins, an inheritance from the time when there were Spanish troops in Fyn during the Napoleonic Wars.

These experiences and sensations conspired to make the 16-year-old boy adopt a radical, revolutionary attitude toward the society in which he found himself. When he went to the university he soon joined the most radical elements, and he caused a quarrel at home when he announced that he could no longer accept Christianity. In every respect he sought to stress the factors which estranged him from society and social convention, and in 1886 he defiantly took part in the workers' procession on Constitution Day. Word of this reached his home, and after the trouble caused two years earlier by his religious views, there were now fresh worries because of his social principles. Those well-meaning, conservative families who had hitherto given him some support in Copenhagen, now refused to help him, with the result that he returned to a life in the capital which verged on dissoluteness. Just how dissipated it was, it is impossible to say—Sophus Claussen said that it was not so bad as Jörgensen made out. Nor is it important to know more about his life at that time; the significant feature is that, as he lived this life, he revolted against it and felt it to be an unworthy manner of living. The traditional moralist within him revolted against the failure of his attempts to establish a new, radical morality. During these years, which culminated in 1889, he had given up his studies and lived as a journalist, first employed by *Socialdemokraten* (*The Social Democrat*), later by *Kjöbenhavns Börstidende* (*The Copenhagen Financial Times*) whose editor was Georg Brandes' brother Ernst. At the same time, in 1887, he published his first volume of poems, *Verse*. In Ernst Brandes' paper he at first made a modest beginning, but then progressed to regular articles on foreign affairs and then literature, making his mark as a literary critic and also producing his own translations of important foreign literature. He appeared to be working his way upward again from the nihilism in which he had been foundering.

In 1891 he married and now began a happy period in his life, his home in Copenhagen becoming a center for literary discussion among the younger generation of poets. Nevertheless, he was too weak to keep entirely away from his earlier life, and gradually his happiness diminished; his wife, he said, only possessed half his heart; he got into financial difficulties; he became so engrossed in his literary activities as to neglect everything else. He edited the journal of the new poets, *Taarnet*, which made great demands on his time and never gave any financial return. There was a religious, even Christian touch about this periodical from the start, and this corresponded with his increasing preoccupation with religion. Indeed, his religious speculations completely dominated his life for a time, putting a stop to his literary production and his work in general. By 1892 he was in financial difficulties again and was forced to move his home. He appeared to be prepared to bring ruin on his family in his desperate efforts to find some tenable view of life, though his attempt to do so merely led for a time to a new form of nihilism. Finally, he was forced to sell his furniture and return with his family to his home in Svendborg.

Before doing so, however, he had met a man whose influence on him was to be decisive for the rest of his life; he was Mogens Ballin, a Jewish convert to Catholicism. Jörgensen always seemed attracted to strong personalities who could help him to form his life. Previously it had been the stoical and proud Viggo Stuckenberg, later it was Andrée Carof. Now Ballin appeared at the right moment. The two had met in Copenhagen and had discussed religious problems, and Ballin, who had set himself the task of spreading Catholicism in Denmark, had seen and understood Jörgensen's predicament. Together with the Dutch artist Jan Verkade, to whom he owed his conversion, Ballin now collected funds so that Jörgensen could spend a period abroad while his family remained in Svendborg.

By way of Berlin and the Benedictine monastery of Beuron he went to Italy, where he stayed for a time with Sophus Claussen. Claussen was not a man to support Jörgensen's increasingly Catholic views, but he left him alone with his speculations. These were accompanied by an increasing sense of longing for his family. It was the first time he had experienced this in all its intensity, but it was to be a frequent sensation in later years. Despite his vacillating character, Jörgensen did not give in to his desire to be reunited with them, and chose rather to transform his longing into a poetical mood; it is as such that these experiences are present in his works, in his lyric poetry as well as his prose. Longing became one of the essential elements in his work, and it was fused with his memories, thus coming to encompass not only distance in space, but also in time. In Pistoja, however, it was physical distance alone which caused him to write a somewhat clumsy poem about his separation from his family.

Still refusing to give in to his desire to return home, he left Pistoja and went to rejoin Ballin in Assisi. It was a meeting and a stay which became decisive for him: "The older I become, the more clearly I understand that that day, and that arrival in Assisi were the basis for all my later life, and that after *la Provvidenza* I owe everything to Mogens Ballin." Thus he wrote to his friend Mogens Kai Nörregaard in 1947.

In Assisi he made his first real contact with Catholicism. Ballin introduced him to a priest, Padre Felice, who made a deep impression on him, and together they sought to give the young Danish poet a living impression of the Catholic faith. For a time they seemed to succeed in bringing him closer to it, but suddenly he experienced a reaction against it, and in October

1894, without having made up his mind one way or the other, he returned to Denmark and to his ruminations. In Svendborg he made renewed contacts with Methodism, but still without feeling drawn to it; in Copenhagen he continued to meditate aimlessly to the detriment of his family life and his finances, but again Ballin turned up and gave his speculations a more positive content. It was doubtless through him that Jörgensen started going to instruction in October 1895, and was received into the Church in February 1896.

In retrospect it must seem amazing that he was able to take this step. During the previous ten aimless years he had shown himself time and time again to be a vacillating character, unable to take a stand, unable to concentrate on his first duty of providing for his family. In addition, the climate of public opinion was averse to Christianity in general to such an extent that the prospect of becoming not merely a practising Christian but a Catholic, would have daunted many a braver man. Yet he took the step, whether or not he fully realized its possible consequences for him, and in doing so showed an impressive strength of character. This strength of character returned to him in his later years and was to remain with him to the end of his life. Henrik Pontoppidan, whose views were entirely opposed to Jörgensen's, once remarked that his conversion to the Catholic faith had given Jörgensen a strength of character which he had entirely lacked up to that time.

There now followed a period of hard work, discipline, and literary production. Jörgensen was appointed editor of a Catholic periodical, *Katholiken (The Catholic)*, an assignment which he undertook with considerable energy, although he used the journal too much for his own private polemics against his former friends, to whom he was now a "renegade," to use Brandes' expression. In 1897 his wife followed him into the Church, and in 1899 they both became Franciscan tertiaries just before they left for Assisi, where he came to feel "at home as nowhere else but Svendborg." Meanwhile he had felt that he had betrayed his social-democratic principles by becoming a Catholic, and although the Christian democratic ideas of Pope Leo XIII overcame his doubts, he was still sensitive to accusations that he was now an "enemy of life," accusations which were apparently made by his wife as well as by his former friends. The mention of such accusations is one of the earliest indications in Jörgensen's autobiography of a conflict developing between him and his wife. In his desperation over the numerous attacks which were being leveled at him, and being depressed by an increasingly difficult situation, he turned for advice to the priest who had instructed him for entry into the Catholic Church, and was told to refrain from all polemics for a period of ten years. This he did. It was a wise suggestion, and it doubtless contributed to Jörgensen's finally being able to continue as a writer.

Since his conversion he had been in grave doubt as to whether he should continue with his literary production. He had felt on the one hand that it was now his duty to devote himself entirely to writing for the religion he had chosen, but on the other he had not felt sufficiently sure of his facts to be able to write subjectively. Thus it has been pointed out that two of his early works, *Roman Mosaic* and *Pictures of Roman Saints,* are among the most impersonal books he ever wrote, completely dependent on the popular, uncritical hagiographies of the day. Jörgensen had accepted the truth of these without even trying to examine the background for himself. He was a poet, filled with an urge to express himself in his writing, but in these books he was unable to do so, and the thought came to him that he should completely give up his literary activities. It was one of the numerous crises in his life at this time, and like the others it left obvious traces on his production. Meanwhile, by chance or by Divine Providence, as he felt it, he found a solution to the problem when he came across an article by a French apologetic, Baudrillart, in defense of complete freedom to study and judge for oneself; even committing errors, Baudrillart maintained, was better than a slavish acceptance of what others had said. This was the lead Jörgensen wanted; it gave him the necessary sense of freedom, allowing him not merely to do his own research and come to his own intellectual conclusions, but also to interpret through his feelings what he had discovered through his intellect.

He was now free to draw on his own entire experience, whether he was writing lyric poetry or the biography of a saint, and it is this which is the characteristic basis of everything which he wrote from this time onward. There has seldom been a writer whose work had a more personal content than Jörgensen's, and the manner in which he succeeded in projecting himself into everything he wrote is one of the most interesting aspects of his art. The first book he wrote after reading Baudrillart's article is of a completely different nature from the previous one. *The Book of the Pilgrim* is one of the most personally charged books ever to come from Jörgensen's pen.

Having returned to Denmark to write *The Book of the Pilgrim,* he also continued his journalistic activities in addition to giving numerous lectures. He began in fact to achieve a reputation in Denmark *despite* being a Catholic writer, and abroad *because* of being one—in Germany Lorenz Krapp wrote an article on him, calling him "der dänische Dichterphilosoph," while in France Téodor de Wyzewa wrote a lengthy article on him in *Revue des deux mondes* in 1904. By 1905 Jörgensen was a regular correspondent of the conservative newspaper *Nationaltidende,* traveling constantly all over Europe for it; his experiences as a traveling correspondent gave him ample material for his journalistic production, and the best of it he later published in book form. Despite all this he was still in financial difficulties, and the tension between him and his wife was increasing: in his autobiography he talks of the years from 1906 to 1909, spent entirely in Denmark, as a period "in God's grindstone." He felt insufficient for his task, and although in the autobiography he assumed the whole blame for the situation in which he found himself, the self-accusations do not ring entirely true. An indication of his real state of mind at the time is to be found on an inscription he wrote inside the front cover of a copy of Huysmans' *Trois églises et trois primitifs* and later pasted over: "Johannes Jörgensen, le 2 mai 1908. Eripe me, Dne, de via iniqua et confirma vitam meam in Te. In Te, Dne, speravi; ne perdet me inimicus!" It says nothing of what he was going through, but it leaves no doubt as to the turmoil in his mind.

In 1909 he was invited to Germany to write the biography of Paula Reinhard. There was money to be earned, but the income from the book had all been spent before he returned to Denmark. He had been well received by Paula Reinhard's family in Germany, but they as everyone else gradually tired of his constant financial difficulties, which were at least partly occasioned by his weakness. His weakness seems to have concerned his wife, and when he met Ballin again, Ballin urged him to take a stand and build up a proper foundation for his life. Exactly

what Ballin urged him to do in practical terms it is not possible
to say, but by 1913 Jörgensen made a clean break with his
wife, and this was followed by civil divorce proceedings in 1915.
Throughout the autobiography Jörgensen indicates that the real
problem was one of finances, but one suspects more than that,
and the fact that his wife left the Church and in fact became
outspokenly anti-Catholic and anti-Christian leads to the assumption that they were also separated by far-reaching religious
differences.

Soon after the break an event took place which was to alter
the remainder of Jörgensen's life. He was invited by the principal of the Institut Catholique in Paris, the same Monseigneur
Baudrillart whose article had had such significance for him, to
give a series of lectures in the spring of 1914. He did this, and
after the last of them he was introduced to a young lady by the
name of Andrée Carof (born 1893), who had heard all the lectures and wanted to meet the lecturer. The two immediately felt
a strong affinity, and a close friendship developed between them.
It was a friendship which led to misunderstanding and much
criticism of Jörgensen, since the two became virtually insepa-
rable. Andrée Carof went to Italy and settled in Siena, where
Jörgensen was then living. She felt he was being exposed to unfortunate influences there, and persuaded him to move to Assisi
in 1915. She also went to live there, and stayed there until her
death in 1933, having a studio in Jörgensen's house, but not living there. In 1921 she accompanied him to Palestine, though in
his book describing his journeys there he never mentions her by
name, calling her instead "my friend the painter," and letting it
appear that his "friend the painter" was a man. The illustrations
to the book were, however, by Andrée Carof, and this was acknowledged.

Every summer Jörgensen and Andrée Carof spent some time
at a house she owned in Velars sur Ouche, near Dijon, and she
accompanied him to Denmark on various occasions; she even
learned to speak Danish, and although they always conversed in
French, she always called him by the Danish term "plejefar"
(foster-father), which in itself says something of the relationship between them. That Jörgensen loved Andrée Carof deeply
is certain, but he once also said that the thought of marriage

would have appeared to Mademoiselle Carof as a "profanation," even if his first wife had not been living.

The relationship between them can best be described as a profound, spiritual union. She was a devout Catholic, and she was the firm, guiding hand he needed. In the past he had not merely experienced financial uncertainties, but he had also been constantly dogged by religious doubts. She overcame these and made him into the devout, unwavering Catholic which he became in later life. Her presence is felt in all the works which he wrote from 1914 to 1934. Jörgensen himself said that she was the prose in his production, though she made no impact on his lyric poetry, an interesting comment which points to an essential difference between his prose and his poetry. Whether her influence on his prose was beneficial or not has often been discussed. To some she was his ministering angel, to others, his evil spirit. Certainly, in the books he wrote toward the end of his life there is a distinct lack of that mental conflict which had made his earlier work so dynamic, and thus from a purely literary point of view there may well be something to be said for the argument that she had a stultifying influence on him. Yet these are the works of a mind at peace, and on a purely human level there is no doubt that this peace was due to her. A judgment of her influence on him will ultimately depend on personal outlooks, but who is to say that her influence on his work should be the ultimate yardstick? Nor would it be true to say that Jörgensen's work from the late 1920s is of little or no value: it is the art of the miniaturist, placid, serene, perhaps not very profound, but beautiful within the limitations he set himself.

In 1933 Andrée Carof died suddenly at the age of 39. Her loss was catastrophic for Jörgensen, and after having a companion with whom he had lived an intense spiritual life, he was left completely alone, without the firm guiding hand he needed. He was by now a famous author, and received a constant flow of visitors to Assisi. Indeed, he was one of the sights there. At the same time he felt himself to be neglected in Denmark, where his poems were acknowledged, but his prose was given little attention, and sales were low. Not even all Danish Catholics appreciated him, and here again he felt slighted. In addition, he began to feel old, and was still a relatively poor man.

After the death of Andrée Carof some of Jörgensen's Catholic

friends in Denmark made an attempt to bring him home and to
have him live in a town in the south of Jutland; but he felt that
this attempt only made more obvious the gap that existed between him and them, and he refused the offer. He felt that they
wanted him home to write propaganda for the Catholic cause
in Denmark: "Naturally the idea is that I should be able to be
of some use. Even when *Journey to Jerusalem* was published
people complained that 'they could not use that book' . . . it is
no text book, no encyclopedia. Now I was to be set in motion
as a traveling propagandist, N.B. at my own expense . . . When
all is said and done, I suppose the fault lies with me in not being
able to cater to the public taste. That Catholics should reproach
me for this is only fitting." [2]

That Jörgensen had misunderstood the intentions of his
Danish friends is obvious, but his reaction to their efforts shows
something of his state of mind. He decided to stay in Assisi and
live there as long as he was able. In his loneliness he wrote
Charles de Foucauld, a memorial to Andrée Carof, which without mentioning her by name is filled with her presence and with
the author's sense of loneliness now that she was dead. Yet in
one way or another Jörgensen seemed to lose contact with his
friends in Assisi; his circle consisted of his landlord's family,
the principal of the Capucin Museum, and a constant stream of
beggars who knew Jörgensen's tender spots and were able to
make the most of their knowledge. There were also the visitors
to Assisi wanting to see the "giraffe," as he put it. The Swedish
writer Ernst Norlind stayed at the house for a lengthy period,
but their friendship evaporated as quickly as it had come, while
Jörgensen went on to take an interest in the petty problems of
various persons of his acquaintance. He was drowning in baga-
telles, he remarked, and could do nothing to save himself. His
contacts with Denmark were slight, and when he visited his
homeland he felt more and more estranged from modern developments there. He was passionately fond of Denmark all his life,
as is obvious from all his work, but Denmark for him was the
unspoiled land of his youth.

Meanwhile he had met a young Austrian lady in Assisi; he fell
in love with her and married her in 1937, his first wife being
dead by now. From this marriage he expected not only personal
happiness, but also a renewal of his creative writing, and he

did produce a book of essays, *The Assisi-Salzburg Axis*, showing something of a return to the German culture on which he had earlier turned his back. Moreover, in his translations of Franz Herwig's novel *St. Sebastian of Wedding* and Papini's *Letters to Mankind* he showed a return to his social Catholic interests which he had largely given up during the Carof period. Nevertheless, his only major work from the last period of his life was *St. Bridget of Sweden*, a project on which he had been engaged for many years. He wrote it largely in Vadstena during the war years, and finished it in Denmark.

After the war he returned to Assisi, but never really settled there again; paradoxically enough, his letters from Assisi show a longing for Vadstena. He seems to have been longing for what was simple and uncomplicated, and Assisi had changed during the war years. Finally, in 1953 he returned to his childhood home in Svendborg which had been arranged for him as a residence of honor. The circle was completed, and he spent his last three years in his old home, dying in May 1956, six months before his ninetieth birthday.

Outwardly Jörgensen's life was not eventful, but inwardly he underwent enormous crises and changes. It is this inner development which places its mark on his work, the change from the fanatical atheist of the very early years to the equally uncompromising Catholic he became toward the middle of his life, the profound mental anguish which accompanied him for about twenty years until 1914 when he met Andrée Carof, the extreme loneliness which was his after he lost her. These are the outstanding features of his biography, without a knowledge of which his work can scarcely be appreciated in all its depth and intensity. Once he had come to an understanding of how he could combine his poetic gifts with his duty to write Catholic works, he proceeded to put himself into his work as much as any poet or novelist writing pure introspective poetry or fiction. The great figures of whom he wrote were interpreted through what the author had experienced, and his own experiences are distinguishable in his portrayal of them; yet at the same time they remain academically sound portraits, not half-fictitious musings. Jörgensen created a new, even unique literary form in Denmark, going much further in his self-identification than for instance Brandes, and constantly seeking parallels between himself and his characters. In the following chapters we shall consider both this new departure and the earlier work in which Jörgensen's originality is equally apparent. And throughout we will be aware of the intense personal implication of almost everything he wrote. Each work can be seen as an identity, a unity in itself; seen in context, however, it assumes a new significance.

CHAPTER 2

The Novelist

L IKE his contemporaries, Jörgensen was at first under the direct influence of Brandes, and his reaction to the Naturalist movement was originally directed against its general grayness and lack of poetic inspiration rather than against its philosophical basis. It was not, then, surprising that Jörgensen should have looked for his prose inspiration not to the mainstream of living Naturalist writers, but to the small production of Jens Peter Jacobsen, who had died in 1885. Jörgensen, the zoological student, was here faced with the work of a botanist; both had something of a scientific training, and both were entirely convinced of the truth of the Darwinist thesis. Yet Jacobsen, for all his enthusiastic support of Brandesian Naturalism, was more lyrical in his approach, more introvert in his attitude to life, essentially concerned with his own private problems rather than with those of society in the abstract, and would therefore automatically appeal to the representatives of a new generation of writers for whom poetry began to take on a new significance.

I Spring Legend (Foraarssagn, *1888*)

Stylistically, the relationship with Jacobsen is obvious in the very first lines of Jörgensen's first novel, *Spring Legend*, with its painstaking description of nature and the final emergence of a man from the scenery, man a part of nature like the trees and the animals. The richly laden language with its piled-up adjectives, many made for the occasion, and the long, complicated sentence structure are strongly reminiscent of Jacobsen. Likewise Jörgensen directly seeks to imitate him in his indications of inherited characteristics and the influence of milieu on the behavior of his main character. Jacobsen had done this both in his two novels and his short stories, and this Darwinist theme is essential

31

to his entire production. In particular, his novel *Niels Lyhne* starts with the background of both parents and an indication of the relationship between them. In a similar manner, Jörgensen introduces a character who, like the hero of Jacobsen's *Mogens*, emerges from nature, and who turns out to be the grandfather of the main character. Thus a brief glimpse of the lives of grandfather and father, of which the first chapter consists, forms a parallel to the similar first chapter of *Niels Lyhne*, and is intended to explain the subsequent career of Jens, the "hero." Both the father and the grandfather have apparently acted according to instinct (another of Jacobsen's themes) in finding wives for themselves, and this serves as a partial explanation of Jens's youthful wanderings from one girl to another. This, at any rate, is the only obvious connection between this first chapter and the subsequent action, for whereas Jacobsen uses his introduction as a basis for what follows, Jörgensen does not. He is content to make a gesture toward the Darwinian, Naturalist view, but emotionally he is far too directly concerned with his main figure to be able to proceed along these lines. He is looking for self-expression, not the expression of a philosophy. And it is Jörgensen's overwhelming need for self-expression which forms the essence of his work and which can be said to be responsible for its strengths as well as its weaknesses.

The story is simple and autobiographical in its essence—the name Jens is, of course, an unused Christian name of the author himself. Jens is given a sheltered upbringing in a small Danish provincial town. He is something of an outsider among his comrades, shy, clumsy, and yet possessed of a sensitive, poetical mind. He falls in love with Anna, but their friendship is a tenuous one, thanks to his shyness and awkwardness. Even when on his last evening at home he goes for a walk with his mother and passes Anna, he is too confused to say good-bye to her. He goes to study in Copenhagen, but is disturbed in his studies by his love of pointless wandering in nature and his longing for Anna, though when he does see her on his holidays he is in any case too shy to speak to her: he feels that his chance of happiness is past. He tries to start an affair with the maid next door, but she is physically stronger than he and puts him firmly in his place. Back in Copenhagen he continues his pointless existence with little work and irregular habits, dreamy meanderings in nature and desperate attempts to find a girl friend, and vain dreams of his successes with them, only to be awakened at the wrong moment by his landlady's harsh voice calling that breakfast is ready! He succeeds in finding a friend of sorts in Jenny, but she is more experienced and wordly wise than he, and she makes greater demands on his finances than he can conceivably bear, and the affair peters out. The story ends inconclusively with his seeing her sitting on a bench in the arms of another man.

It is a short novel which seems to lead nowhere, yet is realistic in its portrayal of the pointlessness of a young man's life just as he is growing up, feeling the desires of late puberty and being incapable of either controlling or satisfying them. He is influenced on the one hand by his physical desire and by his pantheistic love of nature, while on the other he is still influenced by the sheltered upbringing and moral outlook of his home. Thus there arises a conflict between his desire to launch himself out into a life without morals or inhibitions, and his inability to do so; it is the conflict between the desire for life and fear of it, and the result is a surface asceticism of a not very convincing kind. When the other students in Copenhagen press Jens to join them in a night out, the temptation is very great, but it is overcome by Jens's fear and shyness: "But Jens defended himself manfully—finally almost frantically, like a woman fighting a seducer. And with an ascetic delight in his heart Jens finally realized they were withdrawing, just as when St. Anthony saw his temptations flee over the desert. On the evening of the party he stayed at home and read *Faust*." [1]

There is a significant measure of self-irony in this episode as, indeed, there is in the novel as a whole (cf. the episode with the maid and the rude awakening from pleasant dreams already referred to), but the combination of fear and sensuous desire producing a false asceticism, is of considerable interest. The conflict between Jens's natural desires and the asceticism produced by his inhibitions is the key to the whole novel, and it is this which is responsible for his behavior throughout. His inhibitions and shyness lose Anna for him, while his unbridled sensuousness turns the maid Franciska against him, and also causes him to make a fool of himself in Copenhagen.

At times his asceticism is even closely allied to sadism. On first learning from his school friends what physical love entails, and realizing how different it is from his own romantic dreams, he looks at the girls whose purity he has hitherto taken for granted, and is filled with a desire to hurt them: "Something rough and wild arose within Jens—he felt the desire to treat one of these young women brutally—to pelt her with filth and scorn —tear her Jezebel's body with zealous hands and let the dogs eat her flesh." [2]

The transition from impotent desire to asceticism and further to sadism speaks of the author's own experience[3] though it also points to one of the main literary inspirations for the work— Schack's *The Phantasts,* to which indeed there is a reference, as though to underline the relationship between the two. It seems likely that through this medium Jörgensen was able to give expression to his own experience of life, although he still felt justified in maintaining in a letter written to Viggo Stuckenberg in 1893 that "it seems to me, though, that the essential part of my books up to now is what I have *not* derived from my reading." [4]

And indeed, even apart from purely stylistic considerations, there is something new in *Spring Legend,* as behind the sensuous urges a certain idealistic longing is expressed through the book's symbolism. It is essentially vague and undefined, emerging as a longing for light and happiness. Sometimes it smacks of escapism. Jens, lonely and filled with melancholy, longs for "the bright forests of Life," and countless times we hear of "the road white in the moonlight" or "the road white with dust" which apparently leads to the longed-for happiness; once it is even "the road white with dust and baked in the sunlight, which ran right into the shining heaven." Everywhere there are roads leading from stark reality away into the distance, and even the idea of distance itself is constantly re-echoed at moments of crisis or great emotion. No fewer than fifteen passages in this short novel end on this note. On the very first page the landscape is described as "a land with sounds from far away and feelings of longing for the distance," while a few pages later there is a reference to "the distant white roads, where the rumbling of a cart paled far away." In this latter instance a new element appears: we are aware of sound in the distance (described in visual rather than aural terms) detaching itself from the surrounding silence. It is a trait found not only in these early works, but throughout

Jörgensen's entire production, and there are instances of it in the diary entries he includes in the autobiography. In general it is connected with pure emotion: longing, melancholy, happiness, loneliness, perhaps even a sense of eternity, and it is significant that it is not to be found in the last chapter, which relates the sordid affair with Jenny and is perhaps the most earthbound chapter in the whole work. There is, of course, no Christian concept in this sense of the eternal, which springs entirely from the author's pantheistic view of life; but the idea of an eternity, even in this context, was obviously of importance to him and may well be of significance for his later development.

As with eternity, so with mysticism. Jörgensen appears to have been receptive to mystical or pseudo-mystical experiences in his pantheistic period, just as he was later to become concerned with true Christian mysticism. The all-pervading sense of the eternal in nature may well be described as pantheistic mysticism, and just as true mysticism is concerned with a direct relationship to God, so here there is a sense of immediate insight into the spirit of nature, especially to be found in the episode where Jens is alone in Dyrehaven, the deer park just outside Copenhagen: "And then it was suddenly as though a wave of something heavy and mighty passed over him like a wind over waving corn, and bowed his head and filled his soul like a sail in a strong wind. A rolling wave of something which had absorbed into itself all the acrid, earthy scent of the fallen leaves and all the wet fullness of germination in the rotting foliage and which was now moving out across summer fields shimmering with heat toward a happiness which was full and laden with crimson." [5]

This is followed by the sense of distance in two separate passages, through which the longing for the eternal and a mystical experience are fused. It is not stated anywhere, either here or in other works, that Jörgensen himself had such sensations, but the autobiographical element in the book is beyond dispute. If we add to that the fact that the autobiography contains various references to mystical experiences both before and after the final conversion, it is not inconceivable that he might have had sensations of this sort. At any rate, his next short novel, *A Stranger*, also contains evidence of the same sort of experience, while nature mysticism is the basis of the third in the series, *Summer*.

II A Stranger (En Fremmed, 1890)

The story of A Stranger is roughly parallel to that of Spring Legend, though the emphasis is slightly different. Anders, a young student, is lonely in Copenhagen, longing for human, especially female, company. He is poor, and largely dependent on the kindness of wealthy, conservative well-wishers, who for their part expect him to develop into a young man after their own hearts. He meets a young girl, Elna, and falls in love with her, oblivious of her ambivalence, and it is long before he realizes, as the reader has done much earlier, that she is little more than a prostitute. He returns to his home town and feels at peace in the country surroundings, until a letter from his landlord arrives, telling his mother of all that has been going on in Copenhagen. This is a hard blow on the mother, and he thus comes to feel an even heavier burden of guilt than he has done so far, and he realizes that he, like his parents, is not strong enough to come unscarred through life.

The structure of A Stranger is simple in the extreme. Although divided into chapters, the story actually consists of four larger sections: the moods and background in Copenhagen; a series of flashbacks showing early days at home and in Copenhagen; the episode with Elna; the subsequent moods and their effect on the home atmosphere. There is no real logical development, even in the central section dealing with Elna, though this comes nearer to a series of connected events than anything else. Indeed, this work, satisfying as it is to read, is an excellent illustration of the fact that Jörgensen is not a novelist in the accepted sense. Rather than a novel it is a series of interrelated moods, illustrated and created by means of various episodes, each with some significance for subsequent developments. Nor is there really any question of a development in Anders' character, and at the end of the book he is essentially the same as at the beginning, though the disappointment resulting from the Elna affair and the disillusionment caused by the letter home and the way in which he has been treated by the Christian, conservative patrons may well be said to have emphasized characteristics which were already there. As the flashbacks in the second section show well, Anders has always had a sense of being inferior to others, self-conscious in the extreme, although this is coupled with a conviction that he is basically made of better stuff, but simply not suited to the world. Thus develops the conflict which is an essential part of his behavior and thus essential to the novel—a longing to be part of the urban life of Denmark, to take part in it and assert himself, together with the knowledge that he is unable to do so, that he is in some way insufficient. This sense of insufficiency is coupled with a feeling of social inferiority when he is dependent on the patronage of others, and the two combine to make Anders a social rebel, a young man who hates everything on which the social order is based. He becomes an anarchist, though that word is never used of him. In short, every time Anders comes into contact with "the world," disillusionment is the result. He is a more fully developed version of Ahasuerus in the poem of that name which Jörgensen included in his collection of poems, *Moods* (*Stemninger,* 1892). Like Ahasuerus Anders is expressly called a child of the night, and wonders what he has been doing among the children of the day.

Anders' struggle is taken seriously if not directly tragically. The ending is melancholy rather than tragic. Yet at the same time there is a good deal of irony in the portrayal. Even at the beginning, when his self-pity is revealed for the first time, it is done in sufficiently strong terms for it to be seen in an ironic light. Likewise, there is irony at the beginning of Chapter VIII which depicts a rainy evening, with Anders walking about, hungrily looking for female company, slowing down or increasing his pace so that he always meets a woman under a lamp where he can see her better. The atmosphere of the evening and Anders' mood are recreated in melancholy tones, but the whole thing is dispersed in a moment when Anders comes to a main road: "Anders hobbled on his heels across Niels Ebbesens Vej—there were holes in his shoes—and he had a bit of a cold and was afraid of getting wet—and there was always so much water in the streetcar tracks." [6]

Comparable effects are achieved elsewhere in the book, notably when Anders goes, after much hesitation, to apply for a grant, and first bows to the attorney's servant, then, on being ushered into the attorney's room, makes a further deep bow—only to find there is no one there. There is a later episode in the middle of his love affair with Elna, when he is portrayed at some length with a severe cold. At the same time the gentle irony is sometimes transformed into biting ridicule. There are various occasions on which Jörgensen not merely portrays Anders in humiliating circumstances, but seems to dwell on such incidents. The episode in which he makes his application for a grant is emphasized to a surprising degree. His meeting with Elna after having lost contact with her for a time is another: his embarrassment is heightened by her obvious reserve toward him as they walk along. It is most apparent when he has been invited to a party to meet his rival, with the express intention that he should be humiliated. When he tries to make a scene, he is shown the door by his colleague Olsen, who has arranged the whole episode. He breaks down and weeps on Olsen's shoulder, only to be pushed out into the cold. This is without doubt the most harrowing scene in the book. The deliberate humiliation of the main character must have been done consciously; it happens too often to be a coincidence, and this again points to the influence of Jens Peter Jacobsen. In his book on Jacobsen, Frederik Nielsen stresses the author's tendency to show his characters in humiliating situations, and from this he goes on to argue that Jacobsen was an algolagnic. Without accepting this latter part of the argument, it must be admitted that there is a disconcerting number of humiliating scenes in his work; it seems to be a literary technique with Jacobsen, and it is not unreasonable to conclude that Jörgensen had learned something of it from him. One of the most notable instances in Jacobsen's work is in *Niels Lyhne*, when Niels, who is in love with Mrs. Boye, finally discovers her to be unworthy of his affections. The situation is slightly reminiscent of that between Anders and Elna in *A Stranger,* and it is precisely in connection with the final break that the humiliation is greatest.

Anders is, of course, like Jens in *Spring Legend,* a descendent of Jacobsen's daydreamer, whose ancestry can be traced back to Schack's novel. He is not an evil character, and even has some idealism about him; he is searching for a new meaning in life after rejecting the faith and moral code he had been taught as a child. Toward the end of the book the simplicity of his earlier life attracts him back, but the work is inconclusive: what looks as though it could lead to a renewed idyl is symbolically shattered by the arrival of the letter of complaint and the renewed feeling of guilt which ensues.

By the end of *A Stranger* no further progress has in fact been made along the road to a solution than at the end of *Spring Legend;* there is the same nihilism, the same conflict between two cultures, the same impossible attraction back toward the nature in which Anders, like Jens, experiences a sort of nature mysticism:

Peace came upon him. A peace as deep as the night, a nameless, silent peace. It was as though the dew from the grass was seeping through his feet, and as though his skin was breathing the marsh haze and all the air of this night, laden with the scent of foliage, acrid from the scent of the earth, spiced with the fragrance of the gardens, and sourish from the breath of the river water.

Suddenly he was transported away from the world and time. Daily life and the ways of men lay like a distant, heavy dream, buried deep in the soft night. Anders was no longer a wretched, impoverished student who must work like others—study for the sake of his examination and his future career, to give his parents happiness and to help them in their need. He was a tree like the chestnuts along the road at his side—a being who drew in water and breathed oxygen and formed wood—a mere process of development without any will, a life which grew and came into being.[7]

In this mixture of nature mysticism and Darwinism, the desire to show Anders' sense of being transported away from reality coupled with the scientific description of the life processes of the tree, Jörgensen is typical of his time and produces a picture entirely in keeping with his own early production as a whole. Amidst all the fantasy there is both here and elsewhere in this work a positive effort to express himself in scientifically accurate terms. For instance, when Anders at the beginning is filled with self-pity and wishes for death, he thinks of all the atoms in his body being released to take up other functions in nature. This is something well beyond the pantheism of the earlier Romantics, however much they had in common in their desire for union with nature.

III Summer (*Sommer, 1892*)

A profound sense of the mysteries of nature becomes the essence of the third of Jörgensen's novels, *Summer,* which is the culmination of his symbolist prose. It can scarcely be called a

novel, and the second half dealing with the love affair between
Oluf and Fru Astrid is more akin to a long prose poem than
anything else, though it is based on the same fragmentary construction as the earlier works. This is, however, preceded by a
series of conversations between Oluf, the hero, and his friend
Albert, in which Oluf expresses his dismay at the pointlessness
of life and the transience of beauty, the latter being heightened
by the realization that the young women around him "within a
short space of time will be as sacrifices on the altar of the
matrimonial Aphrodite." In addition, their conversations range
over many aspects of literary appreciation and tell of the influence of literature on their lives, especially on that of Oluf,
who admits seeking "a solitary, silent and melancholy place, an
asylum far from the world for one who only wishes to reflect and
dream and write poetry." [8] He is looking for a Nirvana.

This introductory section is much longer than the corresponding parts of the earlier novels, and is undoubtedly tedious in
many respects. The modern reader has difficulty in accepting
the conversations at their face value, just as he might hesitate
to accept the viewpoints expressed as being worthy of serious
consideration. Nor is it the language of a conversation, but of
a correspondence: some of the passages are direct quotations
from letters which Sophus Claussen, who is the model for
Albert, had written to Jörgensen, while Oluf's opinions are doubtless those which Jörgensen himself had expressed, or could have
expressed on paper. We are thus forced to accept the realism
of these conversations to some extent, and likewise on reading
the work as a whole we come to accept the necessity of them
as background for Oluf's affair with Fru Astrid, which forms the
second half. She seems to fulfill the unrealistic and yet sensuous
dreams of Oluf, and to offer him something above the ordinary
run of female acquaintances.

There is something completely unreal about this short-lived
love affair between the young dreamer and the twenty-six-year-
old widow whom he meets during the period of full moon. Ecstatic outbursts such as are not seen in any of Jörgensen's other
writings are found in the chapter entitled "Moonlight," in which
Oluf meets Fru Astrid and under the influence of the moonlight
falls in love with her, while she tells him the story of the moon
prince who vainly tried to entice the young girl to cross the

swinging bridge and go with him to his country in the realm of moonlight. The girl does not dare to follow his bidding. As she tells this story Fru Astrid herself becomes Artemis, the moon goddess. That night Oluf dreams ethereal dreams of walking on "the swaying silver of the moon bridge" across to Fru Astrid, who is again identified as Artemis. It is a dream bathed in a magical light of silver, mother-of-pearl, and white, and the events of the evening are magnified in the bright light of the full moon.

From the magic of the moonlight the work proceeds to the magic of the sunlight, and the next chapter takes place on a calm sea in brilliant sunshine. The supernatural is again mentioned in connection with the legend of Agnete, who married a merman and went to live at the bottom of the sea. In time she heard the church bells of her native town, and asked her husband's permission to leave him and the children for a short time. The permission was given, but when Agnete arrived home, everyone shunned her; even the pictures on the walls turned from her, and she died of remorse. Both Oluf and Fru Astrid consider Agnete's fate to be enviable, for despite the final tragedy, her experience had gone far beyond that of ordinary existence: "For she went to the bottom of the sea and saw all the marvels of the deep and wandered through the infinite forests of seaweed where live the strange creatures which fisherfolk catch in their nets. The deepest parts hide sunken ships and sunken treasures and sunken towns whose church bells ring when the sea is calm." [9] And at these words, real bells are heard to ring: " 'The bells at the bottom of the sea', said Fru Astrid in a quiet, almost inaudible voice."

Gradually Fru Astrid, who is only seen in full stature in scenes such as this where the mysterious and supernatural dominate everything else, becomes the only true reality for Oluf. However, the spell is broken by Fru Astrid's friend, Laura, who is her direct antithesis, lively and extrovert, a child of this world, a representative of life. Similarly, it is she who interrupts Oluf's dithyrambic words on the magic island of love, while Oluf sees, or thinks he sees, on Fru Astrid's lips "the ripple of a smile mocking and at the same time forgiving her friend."

The sense of ecstasy is maintained in the following chapter, this time again in the moonlight, with numerous references to "the market square, white in the moon," and "the road, white

in the moonlight." The awareness of distance is again apparent
in a phrase containing all the most important symbols from this
period, when the author talks of hearing "the soughing of the
poplars in the gardens and the rumbling of a carriage far out
in the countryside white in the moonlight, far away on distant,
unknown roads." Then follows the beautiful scene in which Oluf
and Fru Astrid declare their love for each other. But during
their next meeting, when they walk along the fjord, looking at
the gardens bathed in the moonlight, we hear that the moon is
waning. And Oluf begins to regret his outburst of passion.

His regrets increase, and the next time he is to meet Fru
Astrid, to say good-bye to her before her departure for Copenhagen, he is filled with doubt and misgiving. They do not in fact
meet. Instead, he stands by the roadside out in the country and
watches her go by. There is no moon. All is completely dark, and
all we have is a glimpse of her as she goes past on the white
road and symbolically disappears into the darkness. She comes
from the darkness and returns to it.

We do learn, however, that Oluf's doubts grow when he later
joins her in Copenhagen; she is out of place there, and he senses
increasingly that she is old and faded. She belongs to nature, and
it is only in the magic of nature that her ethereal being can
have any effect on Oluf; she is a child of night and cannot thrive
among the children of the day to whom he has led her. Oluf,
too, is a child of the night, but he longs for the children of the
day: "He longed for all these women who were not his—those
lips he could not kiss—those arms which were not embracing
him—those young bodies which he did not possess—as Tann-
häuser from the delights of the Venusberg longed to love the
maidens of earth." [10]

The apparently supernatural aspects of Fru Astrid are directly
indicated here, just before her final departure for Copenhagen;
but she is not Venus. She is rather the elfin maid of the ballad,
seeking to entice the lonely knight, and it is scarcely a coincidence that the name of Oluf is that of the hero of the ballad
Elverskud, which tells how a knight is seduced by an elfin
maiden. The hero of the novel, like the Oluf of the ballad, experiences the conflict between the natural and the supernatural,
and they both reject the supernatural. The difference lies in the
fact that the fairy of the novel falls in love with him and has

to follow him, whereby she meets her fate. In this she resembles Agnete. She, too, tried to follow her lover from one element to another, with tragic consequences.

Nevertheless, for all these indications of supernatural characteristics and strange ecstatic states, Fru Astrid is a perfectly normal human being, and her supernatural self is merely Oluf's conception of her in certain circumstances. Her mysterious beauty emanates from Oluf himself and is a product of his sensual longings under the influence of certain types of natural scenery. When these particular nature effects are absent, he sees her in a different light, while the reader from the start has been aware that she is considerably older than Oluf—twenty-five or twenty-six. After his passionate declaration of love, Oluf feels as though he is waking after chloroform, as though he has had no control over what he has been saying. He feels that he has been a prey to his own instincts, and knows that he is not capable of loving, as he has professed. Later, when they are out in the country together, away from the more mysterious and sensual aspects of nature, his feelings are again different, and he notices that her kisses taste of sandwiches and wine. Later, in the same scene, he sees her as being "an over-ripe fruit, juiceless and mealy." These are the feelings of a young man looking more or less soberly at the woman with whom he is conducting an affair. Without the magic of nature she is nothing to him, even if, as Albert says, "she is a soul longing for the unknown." The superb symbolism of the entire book merely depicts more forcibly than a realistic portrayal could have done the extent to which a young man's feelings are attuned to the moods of nature.

If the symbolical superstructure is removed, the problem is essentially the same as that in the two preceding novels—the question of a young man's attitude toward the reality which repels him and from which he cannot escape. But he is no longer the nervous young man with a sense of his own inferiority; for despite his obvious loneliness in Copenhagen, he feels himself superior to those around him. Yet his search for a meaning in life leads nowhere, and he is unable to find anything but Nietzsche's idea of an eternal repetition: "I don't know whether you feel it in the same way—but when I look back over the paths I have trodden in my life, they all seem to be without end, leading round and round—always back to the same longings

and the same moods, the same places and the same people. . . .
Has life not brought me back to this fjord which I left seven
years ago? . . . And how quickly have those years passed . . .
and how I have wasted them in the trackless forests of life." [11]

These thoughts are expressed in one of the many conversations
between Oluf and Albert in the first half of the book, and are
exemplified in the second half. The summer's affair with Fru
Astrid again leads to nothing, and at the end Oluf is in more
or less the same position as at the beginning, looking forward to
the next summer, and presumably another repetition. Meanwhile,
the conversations take place on the balcony of Albert's house,
from which the two young men can sit and watch life pass by,
yet being secluded from it—another example of the many symbols in this work. Albert talks continually of his monastic existence, and the idea of withdrawing from active to contemplative
life is common to both of them, though for Oluf life has too
many attractions. Although the conflict between attraction to
and repulsion from life has been seen in the previous novels,
its expression is more pointed and precise here, probably due to
the influence of J. K. Huysmans' novel *A Rebours* which had
served as a model for Jörgensen. In that novel Des Esseintes'
desire to withdraw from normal life is an essential element, while
his reflections on French literature are paralleled by Oluf's and
Albert's conversations on literature to which reference has already been made. In the latter part of Jörgensen's book the
subtle recreation of mood through nature effects is an attempt
at paralleling the fantastic flights of imagination and the taste
experiments to be found in Huysmans' novel. Even Des Esseintes' delight in the strange fancies of artists, his love of
"breathtaking pictures of bandits and succubi, devils and dwarfs,
witches riding on cats and women trying to pull out the dead
man's teeth after a hanging," [12] recall Oluf's memories of his
childhood delight in sadistic stories of brutality and sex. The
difference is that while Huysmans is portraying an unusually
sensitive and degenerate type, Jörgensen deals with something
much closer to everyday reality, the problems and fancies of late
adolescence.

A further point of contact between the two works, though it
may well be coincidental, is the fact that Huysmans' book is a
transitional novel, written shortly before his return to the Cath-

olic Church. It is not Catholic in content, but shows the futility
of a life based on self-indulgence; and the need for a more
positive standpoint is an obvious implication. In *Summer,* too,
there is a sense of futility, apparent in the conversation quoted
above, and equally so in the entire train of events in the second
half of the novel. Oluf knows that his life is empty and that
he has wasted it; and in this he shows signs of an ethical awakening. After his declaration of love for Fru Astrid, it has already
been seen that he feels a reaction against what he has said;
furthermore, we are told, "It was as though he feared some
punishment, as though he had come into conflict with something powerful in existence, with *God*—as though he were break-
ing the laws governing his life." [13] Oluf has a definite ethical
sense, but as yet he does not know how to channel it, and no
solution to his problem is indicated anywhere in the book.

An interesting comment on this, and on the attitudes of
Oluf and Albert (in view of the fact that they are modeled on
Jörgensen himself and Sophus Claussen), is contained in a letter
which Jörgensen wrote to the philosopher Harald Höffding in
November 1892:

> I have just now made the first start on a new book—a bigger and
> better book than any of the earlier ones. And my intentions with this
> new work are expressed in your words on the depths of life, on what
> is *fundamental* in existence. I am about to embark on the great funda-
> mental themes.
> During the autumn I found some support for this in reading
> Schopenhauer's main work. Does that sound strange? But it almost
> seems to me that there is an epic in *Die Welt als Wille und Vorstel-
> lung.*
> While reading it I have incidentally noticed that the two young
> men in *Summer*—if you remember there were two—personify, as it
> were, the two ethical conceptions which exist according to Schopen-
> hauer. Oluf is the affirmation . . . of the will to live, Albert the
> negation.[14]

IV The Tree of Life (Livets Træ, *1893*)

Jörgensen's letter to Höffding seems to indicate an increasing
consciousness on the part of the young author of the ethical
import of his work. It appears that by the time he wrote his next

book, *The Tree of Life,* he was much more positive in his aims than he had been before, and that it was in part due to Schopenhauer that he had reached this stage. Curiously enough, this coincides with a remark by the critic Valdemar Vedel that *The Tree of Life* is less honest than Jörgensen's earlier work. The charge of dishonesty is a serious one, and it may well have been occasioned by a personal disagreement between Vedel and Jörgensen. The book is honest enough, but it is less immediate, more contrived than the others, because by now Jörgensen knew what he wanted to show. It is a *roman à thèse,* as are all his novels from this time onward, and they all suffer from it. At the same time, Vedel is perfectly right in his criticism of the book when he argues that Jörgensen is incapable of making an organic whole of the various episodes in *The Tree of Life.* Whereas previously he set out to depict a number of static experiences, or lives which developed along clear-cut lines, he now tries to show a man who changes, who realizes where his life is leading him and seeks to alter it, even to transform himself. A revolution of this kind is something he had not attempted before, and he certainly failed in this first attempt.

The book is divided into a series of short, clearly defined sections, beginning with an allegory telling of the tree of life which tempts passers-by with its beautiful appearance, but if they come too close it will kill them. Book One tells of Aage's youth at home, his being sheltered by loving parents when he preferred to occupy himself with reading and lonely pursuits. He is intelligent, but develops into a daydreamer, dreaming "visions of heathen bliss and pagan sunshine—visions which shone out against a dark background of vain desire, fine white temples radiant against the dark pine forest." [15] He is to go to Copenhagen to study. Before he leaves, his mother suggests he should receive Holy Communion together with his parents, but he refuses, thus signifying the break with his childhood upbringing. On arriving in Copenhagen he still refuses to commit himself to an active life, and prefers instead to live according to his feelings and dreams, and to write poetry. By the time Book Two starts, Aage has met Niels Graff, a poet for whom Viggo Stuckenberg is the obvious model; together they cultivate a sort of stoical pantheism, though Aage is at the same time attracted by Agnes Graff, the wife of the poet. Graff publishes his first book, in praise of the liberation of mankind, and he also tells Aage that he does not feel bound to his wife: in a free relationship such as theirs, they must both be free to leave the other if they feel so inclined. Book Three, "Refugium," shows Agnes Graff and Aage on close terms, but when Aage boasts of his flirtations with others, she calls him a worm and breaks with him. Aage realizes he could have won her, and in his despair he enters into a series of doubtful relationships, once with a Norwegian girl, Dagmar, once with a barmaid. He realizes that the path he is on leads downward, and he decides he must stop and fight the demands of his senses. However, he meets Dagmar again and strikes up the relationship with her afresh. Niels Graff is reintroduced just as he is about to leave for Paris—his marriage has been a failure, as indeed is his entire personal creed: "I am a Darwinist and a decadent. I believe that what is brutal shall live and what is beautiful die. In the fight for survival between the social organisms called states, the most brutal survive, and we see doomed to extinction those with the noblest souls who strive to attain the heights." [16] His words reawaken Aage's ideals, but the work finishes with his being called to bed by Dagmar. Finally, the short allegorical postscript shows a man bound in a subterranean chamber awakening and spending the rest of his life freeing himself from his chains.

This plot entails a more complicated development than any of the previous ones, notably on account of the change which takes place in Aage. But it comes too suddenly—in a flash— while he is on his way home after a drunken bout in Dyrehaven and sees two children in the same railway compartment as himself. Here Jörgensen should have studied Jens Peter Jacobsen's *Mogens* more carefully. The story is almost a parallel to it: Mogens, the dreamer, loses his wife in a fire and resorts to a wild and dissolute life for a time, finally making a stand against it. But the entire development is much more carefully planned and initiated; it is possible to follow every new direction Mogens takes, and his final stand thereby becomes acceptable. Aage is a completely different case, and Jörgensen is more concerned with brief indications of stages reached; the final episode with the renewed contact with Dagmar is doubtless intended to symbolize something of the struggle going on within Aage, but this is not stated in any clear terms.

Like the earlier works, *The Tree of Life* deals with the conflict between different ways of life, with Aage's attraction toward sensuality and his increasing revulsion against it. But the antipathy now becomes more than a mere instinctive feeling and finds expression in thoughts of guilt and sin. The ethical problems are becoming increasingly Christian in the mode in which they are expressed. In *Summer* Oluf has a feeling, with religious overtones, that there is something wrong with his actions, but here it is expressly stated that Aage "felt sick unto death—as though crushed by some irreparable guilt," and later that he saw "that the world was eternally to be in the power of the flesh and of sin." The feeling of guilt which Oluf has toward Fru Astrid now emerges in a completely different form; from a vague feeling it has developed into full consciousness. The earlier characters have looked for a meaning in life, but Aage is on the point of finding one. He views life clearly, in full perspective, sees his own role in it hitherto and is forced to exclaim, in the words of St. Augustine, "Lord, Lord, how much longer." With these words a new phase in Jörgensen's production is introduced. He has progressed from a purely psychological approach in *Spring Legend* to an ethical viewpoint in *Summer,* and now to a religious basis. The feeling of sin and guilt finally overshadows everything else in this work, and Aage is seen as "a poor, deserted child, whose straying soul had only one desire— the peace of forgiveness which is beyond all understanding." In the final allegory, the bound man finds a lamp burning continuously in his chamber, and the tools necessary for his release are within reach, only waiting to be used; thus we begin to see the solution toward which Jörgensen is gradually moving.

V   Homesickness (Hjemvee, *1894*)

From this it could be expected that his next book, the very short novel *Homesickness* from 1894, would continue the obvious trend toward a religious solution. In fact, however, the solution reached is an ethical one, the return of Glob to the premises of his childhood. As a child he had loved Anna, but he has lost touch with her after going to Copenhagen to study. On returning he finds that she has left her former home, and only by chance does he meet her again in Copenhagen, when she is engaged to someone else. During a further holiday at home he again meets her, re-establishes contact and wins her back, and the book ends with their departure together for Copenhagen. *Homesickness* closes the ring, or perhaps sums up the entire development indicated in the preceding novels, and it is significant that the name of Glob's sweetheart, Anna, is the same as that of the corresponding figure in *Spring Legend*. The provincial setting is the same, and so are some of the memories of childhood, as for instance that in which Glob meets Anna in the churchyard. It is obvious that this short novel is to symbolize the end of the struggle now that the author is on the point of reconciling himself to a new view of life.

On the other hand, *Homesickness* contains no trace of a more positive expression of Christianity. Words such as soul and eternity are frequently used, but they are not directly connected to a Christian view of life. The question of the meaning of life is touched on again, however, and this time it is presented as a question which demands an answer and can no longer be ignored:

Why did this lane, these flowers, these bushes exist? Why did the forest exist, and the clouds and the sky? Why was he himself alive, and why should all this continue thus throughout all ages?

For a long time he had avoided these dreadful questions, which had so often forced themselves upon him in the woods here. Now, like robbers, they sprang from their ambushes and took his happiness from him.[17]

Happiness in the sense of sensuous, heathen happiness disappears; there is still a trace of pantheism and nature mysticism, but it is far less than before, and many of the nature descriptions are there for their own sake, not as pantheistic symbols. The book leaves the reader with a feeling that a solution has been achieved.

Jörgensen's final acceptance of the Catholic faith in 1896 brought about quite a noticeable change in his work, and while on the one hand there emerge signs of the writer into which he was later to develop, there are numerous reminiscences of his earlier work as a novelist, reminiscences which indicate an attempt to use the old literary forms in the service of a new cause. In the very year of his conversion he had written a novel called

Grass, although he did not publish it until eight years later, and in addition he produced several other novels and stories which in part are a development of the symbolist novels, and in part an attempt at a longer, realistic, contemplative novel. None of these works is of outstanding value—though the long *Our Lady of Denmark* (1900) is of considerable interest—and taken as a whole they show that after his conversion Jörgensen was finished as a novelist. The earlier stories had vibrated with conflicts of various sorts due to their being written while the author was experiencing within himself conflicts similar to those on which the books were based, and without his knowing what the outcome of his struggle was likely to be. The strength of these novels lies in their immediacy and in their genuine expression of conflict. But now, in 1896, the struggle is past, and in depicting the same young man in some of the later works, the author is no longer able to impart the same urgency, the same tension, because he no longer feels it within himself. He has made up his mind and tries now to use the young man's problems to the advantage of Catholic moral concepts—the only aspect of Catholicism with which he is concerned in his work at this period.

VI Grass (Græs, *1896, published 1904*)

Grass occupies a rather special position among these works. The plot is largely the same as that in *Spring Legend*, although the names are different and the story is told in the first person. It takes place in Svendborg for the most part, and although the town is not named, the Bagergade and Fruestræde of the book are identical with those of the town, while the storyteller's home is beyond doubt Jörgensen's own. Again the author's childhood is recalled, his fear of his friends, his fear of life, his "strangeness" because he would rather read than join in other activities, his clumsiness and his feeling of inferiority when he falls in love with the prettiest girl in the town. Nevertheless, one essential difference is his attitude toward his own family. In *Spring Legend* Jens is reticent and unapproachable, misunderstood and suspicious of others. On his return home from Copenhagen he finds the whole family gathered to meet him, but he does not appreciate it:

And then to round up the entire family just because he was coming
home!

He went in front of them with his knapsack. It seemed to him that
all the houses in the street were so low that he could see over them
if he stood on tiptoe. . . .

After supper his mother made coffee, and they drank it out in the
summer house by the elder tree. Jens answered the many questions
sharply and briefly, and pushed away the little ones who wanted to
be dandled on his knee. He must be tired from the journey, his mother
remarked: let us not bother him.[18]

However, it is not tiredness but rather his rootlessness and
his longings which have taken hold of him, while the feeling
that the houses were so low indicates a certain condescension
now that he has been in the capital. The same homecoming is
described in *Grass,* but in very different terms:

Dusk was already beginning to fall as the train pulled alongside the
familiar platform (but how small it had become), and the lamplighter,
old Smith with his limp, was already trudging through the streets
when I strolled home at Mother's side along the road I knew so well.
(But how small the houses had become—I could almost see over
them!) My sisters were at the door looking for us: "There he is, there
he is," they cried, and ran down the road to meet us.[19]

This description is radiant with the delight in coming home,
and the remark about the small houses (not *low* as in *Spring
Legend*) is indicative of the same emotion. Similarly, he talks
about the kindness his parents and sisters show him when he
comes home after losing Agathe: "At home they were so pleased
to see me and kind to me, and I reciprocated their feelings, I
suppose—but I still felt a painful void within me." [20]

Eight years separate these two descriptions, and in the mean-
time the author has developed from the defiant radical to the
newly converted Catholic looking back at his youth. Perhaps he
felt he wanted to make amends for some of the things that he
had said in the earlier work, though there can be no doubt that
in *Spring Legend* he showed what he felt at the time. Yet there
may well have been another reason for writing two books so
similar in content. *Grass* does indicate this. The storyteller does
not merely think back on his youth, but he relives it with an in-

tensity for which external factors are responsible. He thinks back on the melancholy of his youth, and he thinks of the German lyric poets he had loved so well: Heine, Eichendorff, Brentano, and Goethe. He compares this upsurge of his former feelings with what is known in German as *Altweibersommer*—"and in the same way I think also that one could talk of an old man's spring. . . . I think it was such an untimely spring which has recently been coming over me now, in my old age. But I also think I have just about written myself out of it in these pages." [21]

These are the words of the author. He, the new convert, is suddenly and intensely experiencing again the feelings of his youth; the effect on him is overwhelming now that he has made a decision to break with the attitudes of his youth, and he is trying to free himself from them. On the basis of this hypothesis this becomes an intensely personal story, almost too personal, and it is without doubt because of this that it was not published when written. By 1904 it would be less likely that the reader would suspect the struggle with which the book is really concerned. That Jörgensen did experience a crisis of this sort is fairly certain, and this little book is the first sign of it.

VII   The Day of Judgment (Den yderste Dag, *1897*)

Compared with *Grass* the story *The Day of Judgment* is impersonal and without a driving force of its own. It loses its power because for the first time the author is using a more or less fictitious plot to show how empty and pointless, indeed even spiritually dangerous, the radical view of life can be, a theme he constantly reverted to in his polemical and apologetic writings from this time on. On his deathbed Niels Graff looks back on a wasted life; he remembers how he scorned the love of a devoted wife in favor of another woman; in his mind he sees how he has failed in all his obligations and only thought of his own fleeting enjoyment and pleasure: "I have hunted the noblest game in the world, and for a time I captured the elusive hind which bounds through the world on golden hoofs, and whose sacred name is Happiness," he says in order to give his life a touch of idealism. Yet now, as judgment approaches, he is alone and has to confess the failure of his life. This he realizes in time to obtain forgiveness, partly through the mediation of the dead wife, Agnes.

Stylistically *The Day of Judgment* is a continuation of the four first novels, and the symbolism at the beginning is strongly reminiscent of *The Tree of Life,* of which it is in any case a sequel. This is particularly obvious in the first chapter where Jörgensen makes the interesting remark that "from the depths of the ego and the senses the elfin mist arises anew, casts its spell on the awakening will, deadens it with forgetfulness, soothes it with dreams and attracts it with longing." [22] Longing, which had been one of the main themes in the previous years, is now condemned as evil. It is portrayed once as an incurable sickness unto death, and when for the first time Niels Graff and Agnes quarrel, Niels watches carefree people passing in the street: "and each of them takes something of his longing with him. They carry his heart away from him bit by bit, until there is an aching void in his breast." Similarly, the symbols which have previously been connected with longing are given a new significance; they come to represent a form of escapism, while their pantheistic aspects also become suspect now that the point of view has changed. The new friends Niels Graff introduces into his home bring emptiness and discontent with them to replace the peace and contentment which had been there before. If no friends come, Niels and Agnes have to go out for entertainment: "But at times their disquiet increases, and their disgust becomes so profound that they cannot be deadened within their four walls. They hurry down into the streets, leave the town, wander about in frosty, moonlight nights along white roads in the deserted landscape until the moon goes down." [23] These are the same symbols as before, but the author's attitude toward them is quite new; he now wants to use them to emphasize the implication of the book, and because of this they lose their poetical effect and are no longer an integral part of the book.

The Day of Judgment is a peculiar mixture of symbolism and realism, in which Jörgensen at times uses a naturalistic manner of writing with a symbolical purpose. This is especially so in the sections in which he employs the most crass realism to portray the horrors of death, the sense of fear which Niels Graff had in his youth when he dreamt he was being buried alive, and his thoughts on the decay which will follow his death:

They were to begin their work, those pale worms. They were to bore into his flesh, on which shaggy mould would soon begin to grow; they were to perforate his bowels, devour his eyes, reduce all his body to an evil-smelling viscous mass in which larvae would develop and swarm and thrive. And when their work was finished they would depart from the mouldy coffin and leave what had once been he, the body with which Niels Graff had lived and experienced pleasure and suffered—would leave it as a pile of brown, defiled bones.[24]

This style is more reminiscent of Zola than of Jörgensen; it is a style he normally left to the Naturalists, and when he uses it here it is with a quite definite purpose, that of describing death in scientific terms and making it as repulsive as possible; this was all the new godless generation could look forward to. The book is a *memento mori,* and in it Jörgensen is doing the same as he had done in some of his minor apologetic works from the same period—using death and the fear of death as a means of converting the wavering.

VIII   Our Lady of Denmark (Vor Frue af Danmark, 1900)

The long novel *Our Lady of Denmark* also has some affinity with Jörgensen's apologetics in its argument that the Middle Ages signified the culmination of Christianity. He had already touched on this subject in one of his shorter apologetic works, *Enemies of Hell (Helvedfjender,* 1898), and had moreover betrayed the source of his inspiration—Thomas Carlyle. He is in particular concerned with Carlyle's book *Past and Present,* which he sees as an attempt to "illuminate the present with the light of the past, to see what is in comparison with what was, in the hope of thus discovering the weakness of our time." [25] In Carlyle's call for a return to a religious basis for life in an attempt to overcome the poverty of the nineteenth century, Jörgensen saw a possible solution to the social problems of his own day, an alternative to the socialist solution which he had favored hitherto, but which he now felt himself moving further away from. Carlyle, he maintains, was "one of the focal points from which a renaissance of idealism and Christianity resulted." There is little doubt that Jörgensen, the significance of his Christian name Johannes (John) not being lost on him, at this time

felt the urge to achieve something similar in Denmark, to be
the voice of idealism in the wilderness of selfishness and brutality.

The influence of Carlyle's thought on *Our Lady of Denmark*
is obvious right from the start, where the young student Herman
Ronge makes a speech at the Student Center and exhorts his
fellows to give up the selfish life they are indulging in and to
return to the "effective and active" Christianity of the Middle
Ages. And Ronge's defense of his point of view is in Carlyle's
tradition from start to finish:

> With some justification you might ask me why I am taking so much
> trouble to conjure up a picture of a vanished age for you. The old
> days are past, and we must live in the century that has been given
> us even if the earth is burning hotly beneath our feet. That is my
> opinion, too; there is nothing I detest more than romantic dreams.
> But nowadays . . . I believe it is up to us to look back at what
> has gone before in order to derive wisdom to face what is to come.[26]

Then he goes on to talk of a rebirth of the medieval spirit,
for, he argues, in the Middle Ages the individual was of greater
significance than individualism, while everything was arranged
according to law instead of license: "The medieval principle was
God's victory over the ego; that of the present age is the liberation of the ego from God." [27]

The novel is an attempt to construct in literature a society in
the twentieth century which has all the good qualities of medieval society. Herman Ronge has been a freethinker and a radical,
a typical representative of his age, but by the beginning of the
novel he has come to see the weakness and pointlessness of the
modern view of life. He leaves Denmark for a period and
stays in southern Germany, reading and studying the works of
Schopenhauer and the French apologetic Ernest Hello. On
Christmas Eve he goes to Midnight Mass in Munich, is overcome by the experience and arranges for instruction in the
Catholic faith; he has been received into the Church by the
time he goes back to Denmark. At home he writes for a socialist
newspaper which nevertheless maintains that religion is a private affair and allows reasonable freedom of expression, and
he comes into contact with a former school friend, Niels Wiig,
now a Lutheran pastor whose social ideas are similar to Ronge's

own. In a lecture given to a Christian students' association
Ronge touches on the work of the English Cardinal Manning,
and points the way to the social Christianity which under the
influence of Pope Leo XIII was spreading over Europe. At the
same time he begins privately to entertain the idea of becoming
a monk and of founding a new order with a social purpose. Yet
he lacks the true humility for this, and when he receives a letter
from Niels Wiig's sister, an atheist, asking him to help her to
a positive faith, he is unable to do so. In order to meditate he
goes to a Benedictine monastery, is overcome by fever and
dreams that he is on the point of death and is damned, but he
is finally saved by calling on the name of Christ. He has come
to an understanding of himself, and he realizes the need for
humility before he can put his grandiose schemes into effect.
He returns home to earn his living as his father's office worker
—the return of the prodigal son. Meanwhile his former editor-
in-chief has committed suicide, and it falls to Niels Wiig to of-
ficiate at the obsequies and to deliver a funeral oration. He refuses to eulogize, and instead uses the case as a warning of the
dangers of the modern way of life. Consequently, when standing at the graveside, he is stoned by the congregation of workers, and is almost killed. Ronge visits him and for the first time
since the letter meets his sister; he asks her permission to hang
a relic of St. Stephen round his neck and to pray to the first
martyr for her brother. In time he recovers, and immediately
asks to see a Catholic priest. Both he and his sister now become
Catholics, while Else Wiig and Herman Ronge are married and
become Tertiaries of St. Francis. Niels Wiig becomes a priest,
and while he is undergoing his training, Herman Ronge, helped
by his father, organizes a "workers' colony," known as Our Lady
of Denmark, which is to be run on Manning's principles and is
to be open to all men of good will, not merely Catholics. The
book closes with the opening of this new venture.

In this book, which must be considered the only Catholic social novel in Denmark, Jörgensen tells the story of his own conversion in broad outline. This is no work of autobiography, but
Herman Ronge is Johannes Jörgensen in essence; he goes through
the same difficulties on conversion from radicalism to Catholicism, even if he does so in different towns and among different
people; the influences on him are the same as those Jörgensen

had experienced. Like Jörgensen he tries in vain to invent a
personalized form of Christianity, while he experiences the same
reaction after being received. Even the great dream has its parallel in the autobiography.

Our Lady of Denmark is an interesting book, of outstanding
importance for an understanding of the young Jörgensen, but
artistically it is not successful. It is an attempt to get away from
the novel form he had practised hitherto and to experiment with
a contemplative, philosophical novel; moreover, it is a realist
novel, very different from the symbolist books of previous years.
Such symbolism as there is, for instance the use of the relic of
St. Stephen to save the life of a man who has been stoned, is
of a very different order. The lack of success is due to Jörgensen's having tried to put too much into the book. He quotes
other authors *in extenso*, a favorite and not altogether successful
technique throughout his life; he recapitulates Ronge's two lectures in considerable detail, and he tries to expose the reader to
as many influences as he himself has experienced. While there
can be some justification for this technique in hagiography, it
is much more difficult to defend it here, as the large number
of quotations transforms the novel at times into a series of chosen philosophical passages all pointing toward Catholicism.

A further weakness is one which has already been mentioned
in connection with *Grass* and *The Day of Judgment:* it is too
conscious, and all the material is used for a distinct and definite
purpose. This leads to a noticeable oversimplification both in
character portrayal and in situation, a fault often to be found
in literature with a social purpose. Herman Ronge himself is to
such an extent identical with the author that he cannot fail to
be convincing as a person, and in this way he continues something of the urgency found in the early novels, but the development in Niels Wiig and even more so that of his sister are too
closely linked to the idea of the novel to carry any conviction.
They are little more than shadows. Similarly, the action itself
is too artificial, although this artificiality does sometimes have
something symbolical about it; the stoning of Niels Wiig has
already been pointed out, but another example is to be found at
the beginning of the book when Herman Ronge is making his
first speech and concludes: "Day and light were promised us,
but we only received darkness and night. . . . My foot is tired

of the paths of night which are slimy like grass snakes and snails to tread upon, and my eye longs for light and sun and day! . . . Let us go out to meet the glow of dawn and to find the day!" [28] —whereupon he walks out of Copenhagen and makes his first, involuntary contact with the Catholic Church.

The scene in the churchyard after Wühler's funeral is decidedly melodramatic in character, while the subsequent semi-miraculous cure which leads to the conversion of Niels and Else Wiig is naive and artificial. But Jörgensen was working toward a goal which he obviously thought he could best reach by these means. The graveside scene has moreover connections with events of the day and with Jörgensen's treatment of them in his apologetic works, as it is a reconstruction of an oration held at the funeral of the dead after a shipwreck off Harboöre. The priest concerned, Pastor Moe, caused a storm of protest, though he was not literally stoned. The newspaper discussion of Niels Wiig's oration is similar to that of Pastor Moe's, while the socialists' pseudo-Christian arguments are very similar to those to which Jörgensen refers in *Enemies of Hell*.

In general it can be said of *Our Lady of Denmark* that it is an attempt to translate into fiction the points of view and the arguments which the author had propounded in the various minor works he had written a short time earlier; there are various reminiscences of essays on *The Papacy and Culture* (*Pavedöm-met og Kulturen*) and *Harald Höffding*, and of *Enemies of Hell*. It is filled with ideas, but artistically it is less than successful.

IX   Eva *(1901)*

Nor was the last of Jörgensen's novels, *Eva*, any more successful, though for a completely different reason. It is more directly connected with the earlier works, and is basically a repetition of *Grass*, and thus a distant relative of *Spring Legend*, though somewhat broader in scope. It tells of a doctor's wife who falls in love with a poet called Bjerre, and, when he leaves his wife, accompanies him to Switzerland. In Lucerne they stay at a strange, dilapidated hotel where they are filled with a superstitious fear of being attacked. In his terror Bjerre prays to a picture of the Madonna for help. No attack is made on them, and Bjerre then leaves his mistress and returns to his wife. By the end of the book both are Catholics. It is a poor book, the best features of which are the descriptions of bohemian life in Copenhagen, which Jörgensen knew well, and which he portrays in some detail. Bjerre, Dr. Foersom and the poet Geismer are all living characters whose variations on freethinking are well depicted. The night of horror in Lucerne appears to be ultimately inspired by a night Jörgensen and his wife had spent in Innsbruck, and which is described in "The Unleavened Bread" in his autobiography. In *Eva,* however, it is more reminiscent of Victorian melodrama, while the subsequent conversion happens without the least trace of preparation apart from the fact that Bjerre had once made fun of another poet for his conversion.

This was Jörgensen's last experiment as a novelist. Prior to his conversion he had been productive in that genre, and despite a certain uniformity had really achieved something. Now he appears to have recognized the impossibility of using this form of literature in order to gain the objectives he had in mind. Instead, he began to look for a new literary form for his gifts and his purposes. Nor was he long in finding it, and thus he began to produce works in the genre which became characteristic of his mature art.

CHAPTER 3

The Early Hagiographies

I *First Attempts*

J ÖRGENSEN'S other prose works from the period immediately
following his reception into the Church were predominantly
polemical. He had one of the best of all Denmark's polemical
pens, and he used it with equal vigor to attack his former comrades in arms and their radical philosophies, and to criticize the
liberal theology of the Lutheran state church, although in *Enemies of Hell* he showed considerable sympathy for the more
extreme evangelical wing, the Inner Mission. Brilliant as these
short works were, they could scarcely have lasting literary value,
and at the same time as Jörgensen was coming to the end of his
career as a novelist he began to experiment with a new literary
form, the biography. The first of these, *An Apostle* (*En Apostel*)
was published in 1900, the same year as *Our Lady of Denmark*,
and tells the story of Father Damien, the French missionary who
devoted his life to the lepers of Molokai.

This was no ordinary biography, but contained a generous
amount of polemics and purely informative passages on Catholic beliefs and practices; Jörgensen was not merely intent on
refuting the ideas of those who thought differently—he intended
to educate his countrymen, too. Meanwhile, in the course of a
hundred pages or so he tells the story of Father Damien's life
of sacrifice after his having given up a more comfortable life
in France. He shows him as having accepted a new sort of reality,
the reality of self-sacrifice. He portrays his arrival at Molokai
without anywhere to live, and tells how he had to spend his
first night under a pandanus tree on the beach. It must have
been a considerable temptation for a writer with a poetical nature like Jörgensen's to dwell on such an exotic scene as this, but

he had begun to change, and avoided the temptation, though not entirely without referring to it:

What thoughts went through Father Damien's soul that first night as he lay under the tree and waited for sleep to come, and listened to the waves of the southern sea rushing against the shore and saw the bright stars of the southern sky twinkling above him? A Pierre Loti[1] would from such moments have produced pages filled with melancholy; he would have heard the sound of the blue carrion-eating crabs swarming among the stones on the shore, and in the somber darkness and the gentle puffing of the breeze he would have sensed the presence of Tupapahu—the ghosts and spirits of the Maori legends. He would have thought of the women he had seduced and deserted and ruined—of little Rarahu from beautiful Tahiti who had died of sorrow and of longing for him—and his pain at his lost happiness and his repentance over the woman who had died for him would have been yet another mood—would have been yet more wine and intoxication in the golden goblet of life. . . .

But Father Damien was no poet, no sentimental, merciless dreamer who saw in the world and in men only food for his hungry soul. He was one of those who *lived*, not one of those who merely *experienced;* he was one of those who gave, not one who took.[2]

If the exotic background of the first paragraph were to be removed, the name of Pierre Loti could be exchanged for that of the young Johannes Jörgensen himself, for it is a description of Jörgensen the pantheist, even containing stylistic echoes of his early work: melancholy poetry, vague melancholy, a sense of the spirits in nature, regret at his ill-treatment of women, the materialistic joy of life. But while Pierre Loti emerges almost as a symbol of the young Jörgensen, Father Damien comes to represent the older man, rejecting the poet's egotistical treatment of life and representing a new conception of reality.

In writing this book Jörgensen had found a certain limited affinity between himself and the man of whom he was writing, and he had managed to express through him something of himself and his experience of life. In this particular work the affinity is taken no further, and it may well have been that Jörgensen paid relatively little attention to this aspect of his biography. Nevertheless, here are the seeds of the later works, the first indication of how he was subsequently to project his own personality into the biography of another man. Elsewhere in *An Apostle* the style is factual, and the only way in which personal feelings are expressed is in the author's obvious admiration for a man who was able to turn his back on the world and live and die among the lepers of Molokai.

It is not clear to what extent Jörgensen at the time realized the potentials of his approach in *An Apostle,* or whether he felt an inherent danger in it, the danger of overstepping what a pious Catholic was entitled to put of himself into a book dealing in one way or another with the Faith. Indeed, so great was this problem for him that for a time he hesitated and debated with himself whether or not he ought to give up writing altogether. At all events, it was not until 1903 that he decided how he could go on writing and still put himself into his work. He discusses the problem and his own state of mind in his autobiography: "Anxious as I was still, and frightened of being on the wrong track, I needed all the assurances I could get. Therefore this book [*The Book of Rome*] goes to great lengths as Catholic apologetics, deriving as much proof as possible from the archeological facts. I zealously wanted to fix dogmas in place with historical four-inch nails, and this eagerness was related to my delight at being able to call myself a 'Christian democrat'. The authority of the Church had not found a natural balance within me, and I still sought to support it with external authorities." [3]

These words apply to both parts of *The Book of Rome: Roman Mosaic* (*Romersk Mosaik,* 1901) and *Pictures of Roman Saints* (*Romerske Helgenbilleder,* 1902), and are also applicable to *The Sacred Fire* (*Den hellige Ild,* 1902). All, however, carry a stage further the technique embarked upon in *An Apostle* and are thus another step in the transition to the hagiography proper which started with *St. Francis of Assisi* in 1907.

In many respects *The Book of Rome* seems more impersonal than others from the same period, but the newly converted author is plainly still concerned with conversion as a phenomenon, as he had been in an earlier volume entitled *Conversion* (*Omvendelse,* 1899). This emerges from the portrait of St. Bridget of Sweden, the central scene of which is that where Bridget cannot sleep and hears the crucifix in her bedroom speak to her. Similarly in *The Sacred Fire* Jörgensen dwells at length on Giovanni Columbini's conversion and seems more directly interested in this part of his story. In a passage of free narrative he shows how Columbini finally makes up his mind after reading the legend of Mary of Egypt, which is one of the stories included in *Conversion.*

The literary form and the essential basis of the story of Columbini place *The Sacred Fire* closer to *St. Francis of Assisi* than any other book Jörgensen had written so far. It tells of a wealthy man, fond of the good things of life, who is converted and then sacrifices everything for his new faith, seeking to spread it by going from place to place preaching and doing good works. As later in *St. Francis* Jörgensen starts with a freely invented episode depicting Columbini's relationship with his wife, followed by his conversion, and throughout this section he is reflecting his own immediate history. The same doubts which are implicit in all that Jörgensen wrote at this period are ascribed to Columbini when he comes after a long absence: "Alas, was he perhaps only an old fool who had thrown away warm, living reality in order to grasp at cold, empty shadows?" [4] he asks himself, spurred to this state of indecision and irresolution by his meeting with what he had known in former times, just as Jörgensen was constantly being undermined in his faith by his old allegiances. Similarly, a feeling of insufficiency expressed after Columbini's quarrel with his wife seems to have a personal implication: "Scarcely had the door closed behind her when it was as though a pain went through her husband's heart. On the one hand he would have liked to give even greater vent to his anger—and now he was suddenly alone and had no one to take it out on. On the other hand he was ashamed at his quick temper —but this sense of shame could not assert itself sufficiently, and so only made him still more bitter, still more angry." [5]

A passage such as this in an impersonal account seems to indicate personal experience both inwardly and outwardly, and early letters and a good deal of the autobiography speak quite plainly of constant quarrels between Jörgensen and his wife. Here, perhaps for the first time, the story does not merely give Jörgensen an outlet for his need of self-expression, as in *An Apostle,* but springs to life and takes on a completely new character.

Freely invented episodes are also used in *Pictures of Roman Saints,* as when St. Peter meets Acilius in Rome. There are some of Mogens Ballin's features in St. Peter, while Acilius, the learned man who has tried all the philosophies of his time in order to find an explanation of life, reminds us in broad outline of Jörgensen, groping for the truth in the days before he met Ballin.

Similarly, the account of St. Bridget's arrival in Rome is connected with an attempt to gain poetic insight into her feelings on this occasion. It is the same sort of technique used forty years later in the full biography, and in general the portrayal of the Swedish saint in *Pictures of Roman Saints* is a sort of early study for the major work, an impersonal study for a personal work, which nevertheless expresses some of the thoughts which were subsequently to become of more importance to Jörgensen—revelations and their role in the history of the Church, and the unity of Europe in the Catholic Middle Ages are two of them. One of the most beautiful passages, a poetical and sensitive description of spring at Bridget's home, was to be transferred word for word to the later work (see p. 147).

These early works of hagiography are not among Jörgensen's major achievements. Despite the features which they necessarily have in common with the rest of his works, they are pale and impersonal, only lit occasionally by glimpses of what is to come. The author is still not master of his art, and it is quite conceivable that his personal knowledge of the subjects he was writing about was very slender indeed, that he was tied to the few books, perhaps even the only book, he had read, and thus incompletely equipped to form an opinion or a conception of his own and to put his personal stamp on it. In addition, if these early sketches are viewed in the light of his known method of working, it must be stated that he simply felt little personal contact with some of the saints he was portraying. The personal conception of St. Bridget on which the later biography was based, could not exist then, while St. Cecilia and St. Agnes are not figures to whom he later returned. Of course, St. Peter occupied a special place for him, but there is nothing to indicate any point of contact between the two—St. Peter had all the qualities Jörgensen lacked. In later years St. Philip Neri is again mentioned several times, but Jörgensen never produced a full-length biography of him, though he did consider doing so. Giovanni Columbini was much closer to Jörgensen, and in consequence *The Sacred Fire* is more alive than the other two books.

However this may be, the ultimate reason for the weakness of these books is that indicated in the autobiography. Jörgensen was simply afraid of writing anything which allowed of too personal an interpretation, afraid of drawing the wrong conclusions. As stated before, his reading of Baudrillart's article in *Le Correspondant* about the relationship between historical research and dogma gave him the freedom he had hitherto lacked.[6] Now he came to feel confident that he could carry out research and produce his own interpretation without any fear of doing wrong, and this gave him the courage to write books reflecting the whole of his personality, not merely a fragment of it. The first result of this breakthrough was the travel book *The Book of the Pilgrim;* the second was *St. Francis of Assisi,* in which Jörgensen's prose art suddenly burst into full flower.

II   St. Francis of Assisi (Den hellige Frans af Assisi, *1907*)

Is it of himself or St. Francis Jörgensen writes when he says of the saint:

For who was he to dare to be a signpost for humanity and the master of disciples, he who, only a few years ago had been a child of this world among children of this world, a sinner among sinners? Who was he to dare to preach for others, to exhort others, to guide others—he who was not even worthy to utter the holy and pure name of Jesus Christ with his impure, carnal lips? When he thought of what he had been, and what he could become again if God did not support him, because at bottom he was still the same—when he thought of this and saw what others considered him, those who honored him, those who followed him, he was filled with horror; then he did not know where to hide himself for shame, then the words of the apostle resounded in his ears: "that I, who preach for others, may not myself be condemned." [7]

The factor which distinguishes Jörgensen's *St. Francis* from so many of the other biographies of the saint is the deep, personal implication St. Francis had for him. He was writing of a man who commanded his deep respect and with whom he felt a special affinity, a man he had a special reason for feeling he understood. *The Book of the Pilgrim* had already shown the intimate feeling the author had for the saint's native country, and his close knowledge of the scene of the action. Here, in the biography, we are not so much concerned with intimacy with the external scene as with the entire range of St. Francis' thought, which is made possible by certain similarities in the two men's mental makeup and in their personal experience. Jörgensen could interpret Francis because he had known enough of such experiences to be able to put himself in his place. Thus, within certain limitations, he can depict St. Francis by putting himself in his place, even going so far as to comment on his "unprepossessing" physical appearance, a trait he had on more than one occasion mentioned in connection with himself. That this sense of affinity was a limited one is indicated by an interview Jörgensen gave to the newspaper *Ekstrabladet* on October 3, 1925. The interviewer asked whether Jörgensen considered St. Francis to be his ideal and received the following reply: "That would be saying a lot—it is something I cannot say. . . . One ought to resemble one's ideal—and that is far from the case here . . . although I strive for it with what little ability I have. But I have always felt a special attachment to *him*—he was an extremely great man."

Nevertheless, the similarities between them are at times so striking that we are reminded of them throughout numerous and lengthy passages; it would scarcely be saying too much to assert that a knowledge of the autobiography is necessary for the personal implications of this work to be fully appreciated. It is an outstanding example of the fusion of scholarship and intuitive understanding which characterizes all Jörgensen's mature hagiography. This is immediately and especially apparent in the fictional introduction which is based on the author's own experience and his relationship to his mother. The tension which becomes apparent between Francis and his mother when she touches on religious themes is that which had arisen between Jörgensen and his mother when he had broken with his childhood faith, a tension which is explicitly discussed both in the autobiography and the early novels. Similarly the description of Francis' sense of fear that his youth is passing may well reflect Jörgensen's own feelings on this same subject, one with which he was very concerned at this period.

The loss of his friends and the doubts subsequent to conversion are reflected in the episode in which Francis is out begging for oil for his church at San Damiano, but cannot persuade himself to visit the home of one of his former friends: "Then his courage suddenly deserted him—he who had defied his father and not feared the robbers on Monte Subasio was ashamed of showing himself before his old comrades! Perhaps he experienced one of those short but so inexpressibly crushing moments which all converts know, when what they have left behind seems to be so clearly and obviously natural, right and reasonable, while the new thoughts and the new life suddenly appear to be acquired, artificial, stilted—something they will never quite master, but always try to force themselves to." [8] This must not in itself be taken as a sign of doubt in the author, but there has been sufficient evidence of such doubt in his earlier Catholic writings for it to become apparent that he is understanding Francis through himself. In every respect the struggle which takes place within a convert is depicted with greater calm than before, and there are even signs that Jörgensen is able to look critically at the way he thought and behaved just after his reception: "But like all men in the beginning of their conversion, the young man immediately thought just as much of others' faults as of his own . . . 'How foolish they are, loving transient things,' he thought to himself with a sort of feeling of superiority as he went in through the gate of the town." [9] Jörgensen's thoughts have obviously gone to his own criticism of his former friends, his lack of understanding of their point of view, and his polemical attacks on them. This book was written during the period when he was forbidden to take part in polemics, and he knew he had benefited from this. Instead of criticism and polemics, Jörgensen's *St. Francis* is characterized by charity and warmth, and time after time the humanity of the saint is underlined. Early in the book Jörgensen talks about the goodness of the Franciscans, while in the long discussion in Chapter viii of Book iii on the various Rules of the Franciscan Order, the author's comments show his enthusiasm for the simplicity and humanity of the saint. The following chapter and its treatment of Francis' antipathy to

learning brings similar traits into the foreground: "Prayer and
life as a whole, not the word or theory became thus the essentials for Francis, despite all; they were of supreme importance
to him and his brethren. Others could go whatever way they
wished; he neither blamed nor condemned them any more than
he blamed or condemned those who went in costly clothing." [10]

Two chapters later Jörgensen speaks of Francis' "infinite
gentleness and tolerance." He was not, he says, the man to "ex-
tinguish the smoking snuff or break the bent reed." It is this side
of him, as well as the deeply religious nature of the saint and
his profound reverence for holy things, that fascinates Jörgensen,
and which seems to be connected with his own sense of social
responsibility.

Yet this warmth and tolerance are qualities which Francis
has had to cultivate within himself; they are the results of his
conversion and of his accepting the discipline of the Church,
even when this was painful to him. He had learned to know
himself (a theme Jörgensen was to deal with more fully in *St.
Catherine of Siena*), and he had achieved a victory over himself.
All this had given him peace, on which Jörgensen significantly
comments: "The first means to achieving peace for Francis was
obedience, which he understood as the complete renunciation
of all selfish willing, complete subordination under every command and every authority." [11] It was what he himself was striving to do.

While the inner experiences of the saint spoke to something
in the poet, the externals of their careers also had a common
element: once having deliberated on their real calling, and having come to an understanding of what it was to be, they saw it
as an outwardly directed activity, Francis in his preaching and
Jörgensen in his writing. To what extent Jörgensen saw his writing as a sort of preaching is implicit in the writing itself; he is
a moralist who never fails to draw the reader's attention to the
moral implications of what he is telling, or to digress from the
immediate account in order to philosophize on its significance.
This digressive tendency is one which comes more and more
into the open in the later works, and which has been criticized
as being irrelevant to the work in hand. While there at times can
be some justification for this criticism, there can be no doubt

that the digressions are intentional and part of the aim to influence the reader and not merely to entertain him, not merely,
even, to give food for thought. On more than one occasion
Jörgensen, with reference to his own Christian name, talked of
himself as another "voice crying in the wilderness," and this,
too, becomes evident in *St. Francis of Assisi* both in the reference
to St. Francis' words "Præco sum magni regis" and later with a
direct reference to John the Baptist in connection with Francis'
outward appearance: "And Francis was an uncompromising moralist. He was never silent about what he felt to be wrong, but
called all things by their proper names. Despite his unprepossessing outward appearance, he thus filled people not only with
respect, but also with fear. There was something of a John the
Baptist about him."

In addition, Francis was a poet, and it is thus not surprising
that Jörgensen allows his book to build up to a climax in Book
Three, "God's Minstrel," in which Francis succeeds in "playing
good folk into heaven" and "filling people with enthusiasm for
God." In this section all the main currents of the work as a whole
come together. On the one hand, Francis' activities reach a climax; he succeeds in his efforts to attract followers, and sees that
his preaching has had the desired effect. Yet in the midst of his
triumph he suffers, and can be presented in a tragic light. He was
no genius at organization, and while his simplicity and earnest-
ness were sufficient to lead his followers while their numbers
were small, these characteristics were not sufficient to lead an
enormous group of followers whose views in many cases were
far removed from what he had originally envisaged. Thus he
came to experience a split within his following, and had to allow
himself to be replaced as head of the movement. There is considerable pathos in Jörgensen's presentation of this dual development, though in the fourth part of the book he finds some consolation in the fact that Francis had always been something of
a hermit and mystic, and in showing that his withdrawal from
the more active leadership of his movement gave him the opportunity to turn to other paths which for him were equally
fruitful. At the same time his poetic gifts emerge in what
Jörgensen terms the "religous poetry" of the Regula Prima, as

he emphatically prefers to call what subsequently became known as the Rule of 1221.

In his efforts to keep his movement to the paths he had originally intended, and understanding the necessity of writing for such large numbers a more precise Rule than he had originally intended to compose, Francis wrote the Regula Prima when he withdrew from active leadership:

> To this belongs first and foremost the *Laude* or song of praise which has already been mentioned, and which Francis had ordered his Brethren to sing in the towns around as good minstrels of God, and in which we find tones reminiscent of the later Sun Song. What Francis wanted more than anything else was to fill people with enthusiasm for God. And after a final *Admonitio fratrum* . . . this work of his and of Caesarius of Speier finishes in a great, swelling song of praise which rises and rises constantly like the ever more powerful surge of an organ, and does not stop until it has reached the highest peak— that point where all human speech must be silent, all human thought must fail, and where nothing is left but the angels' *Sanctus, sanctus, sanctus* and the saints' unending *Alleluja*.[12]

And after this dithyrambic introduction, doubly striking because of the relative lack of emotional language, Jörgensen furnishes an impeccable and beautiful Danish translation of the final pages of the Regula Prima. The poet has got the better of him, and the poet within him must break forth and express its admiration and enthusiasm for the poetry of the saint. There are few such moments in the book, few occasions when Jörgensen does not keep a strict control of his language, thoroughly chastened as it is after the emotive manner of much of what had been written before. Even the description of the hermitage of La Verna is remarkably subdued if compared with the related section in *The Book of the Pilgrim*. There Jörgensen had given expression to his own lyrical feelings, and put the description into the mouth of a Franciscan monk, Father Samuel: "What a place in which to say Holy Mass. . . . Just imagine the mornings which Brother Leone and St. Francis experienced there together—the one standing in front of the altar, the other at its foot. . . . Far below them in the valley, beneath the violet mists of morning the world slumbering still, and high up in the mountain that miraculous act in which God Himself becomes present for us in the white Host and the consecrated chalice." [13] In *St. Francis* this passage is condensed to a mere: "Brother Leone's grotto high up on the mountainside, where Francis many an early morning was present at his friend's Mass and adored the Body and Blood of God in the white Host and the golden chalice." [14]

In general, Jörgensen simplified and abbreviated to a large extent the passages which he took over from the earlier book. An instance of this is the episode where the grapes in the presbytery garden in La Foresta are spoilt by a crowd of people wanting to see Francis, who then has to make amends to the priest. Francis' departure from La Verna is another, despite the emotion still remaining in this passage. An interesting exception to this general trend is the account of how Brother Leone found Francis deep in prayer in La Verna; in *St. Francis* this is certainly shorter than in *The Book of the Pilgrim*, but as the poet retells the story from *Fioretti* in his own words, his delight at the moonlit landscape is nonetheless so great that this aspect of the scene is emphasized more than in the original. Here we can justifiably talk of Jörgensen's being carried away by his lyrical enthusiasm and thus producing a passage reminiscent of the many moonlit landscapes in his earlier work.

The author's love of nature does become apparent throughout the book, though this, too, like the lyrical language which is so closely associated with it in the early Jörgensen, is less immediately obvious than previously. The potential for nature description in a book whose action takes place in the midst of such scenery is very great indeed, and there are countless occasions on which Jörgensen could have indulged in sounds amidst silence, or roads winding and disappearing into the hazy distance; yet they are almost entirely absent. Jörgensen has been rigorous in his demands on himself to produce an unemotional description of nature. Thus the effect is in fact far greater when, in a few passages like the moonlight scene referred to above, his old skill at nature description is given free reign. It happens again in one final, emotional episode when Francis is being taken to Portiuncula to die, and as he is being carried away from Assisi for the last time, asks to be turned round so that he can see it:

For a moment there was a profound silence while the sick man was raised up with the help of the Brothers. Up on the mountainside lay the walls of Assisi and its gates and row upon row of houses gathered around the towers of San Rufino and Santa Maria della Minerva. Above the town towered the naked mountain with the ruin of the German castle at the top, as it does to this very day. Further away Monte Subasio showed blue; there lay Carceri, and at its foot San Damiano lay hidden. And between Francis and the two was the great plain where as a young man he had ridden his lonely rides and dreamed of achieving great things.[15]

Doubtless Jörgensen felt attracted to St. Francis because of the saint's love of nature, but he felt obliged in this connection to assure the reader that Francis' attitude was a different one from the pantheism he himself had once professed:

To understand the Sun Song we must understand Francis' attitude to nature. Nothing would be further from the truth than to call him a pantheist—never does he confuse either God or himself with nature, while the pantheist's contrasting moods between orgiastic intoxication and pessimistic horror are quite foreign to him. Francis never wished with Shelley to become one with the universe, nor did he with *Werther* or Turgenev tremble to feel himself a prey to the inexorability of things and the "eternally ruminating monster" that was nature. Francis' attitude toward nature is entirely that of the first article of faith—he believes in a *Father* who at the same time is a Creator.[16]

From this point of departure Jörgensen goes on to point out how Francis saw all men and women as his brothers and sisters, how he loved to see the promise of nature against this background—"light and fire, clear, running water, flowers and birds." Part of his attitude was conditioned by the religious symbolism he himself saw in the things of nature: water reminded him of baptism, for instance. This pure joy in nature was the opposite of Jörgensen's own in his early youth, and he doubtless spent much time discussing it as a counterweight to what he had said in earlier works. It is scarcely possible to imagine a greater contrast in attitudes to nature than that of Francis as here presented, and that which Jörgensen shows in *Summer*. Here, too, is doubtless the clue to the main reason for the unadorned style of *St.*

Francis; there is a conscious effort on the part of Jörgensen to distance himself as much as possible from the past, and to emphasize the change in his outlook. Stylistically it is a stark book, and the bareness of the descriptions and of the language in general is not paralleled in the later hagiography. Having once made the break with the past, Jörgensen seemed later able to relax, stylistically speaking, and take more liberties than he did in his first major work of his Catholic period, though never did he return to the florid style of former years.

St. Francis starts by showing the convert, and goes on to portray the builder of churches when Francis takes his task of rebuilding churches quite literally. At the same time he has a social duty, to tend to the poor and the needy. He is later portrayed as a preacher and leader, and finally, after withdrawing from his active life, as a mystic. All this corresponds to some extent to something in Jörgensen himself, and the way in which the book closes on the theme of mysticism is a fitting introduction to an increasing interest in Christian mysticism in general in subsequent books—in the figures of Suso, St. Catherine, and St. Bridget. This biography thus covers an enormous development, all of which corresponds to something within the writer himself. However, the treatment of mysticism, centered on St. Francis' life in La Verna and the subsequent stigmatization there, is much less penetrating than in the book about St. Catherine. Franciscan mysticism was much simpler than St. Catherine's because, as the episode in La Verna stresses, St. Francis wished to keep his experiences to himself. He even tried unsuccessfully to hide the stigmata.

Perhaps it is precisely this factor, the relative lightness of touch in dealing with mystical experiences and their expression, which makes *St. Francis* the most immediately attractive of Jörgensen's three major hagiographies. It is carried along by the enthusiasm of the author, and by his stress on the simple virtues and the warmth of the saint—a very different story from what he was to find some years later when he turned to St. Catherine. In its perfect fusion of scholarship and legend, of poetical beauty and simplicity of expression, of profound feeling and clarity of presentation, this book is unique in Danish literature.

III   The Loveliest Rose (Den yndigste Rose, 1907)

For Jörgensen 1907 was an important year. Apart from *St. Francis* it saw the publication of one of his major collections of lyric poetry, *Flowers and Fruits* (*Blomster og Frugter*), as well as *The Loveliest Rose*, a book on the life of the German mystic Heinrich Seuse, otherwise known as Suso or St. Amandus. It is scarcely possible to think of a greater difference in the manner of presentation than that between *St. Francis* and *The Loveliest Rose*. In the latter book Jörgensen ventured into new fields, into the sphere of Dominican mysticism, which in turn has connections with Franciscan mysticism. From this we have a direct line to St. Catherine of Siena, who stood in close relationship to the Dominican Order. Also, the new book is a contrast to *St. Francis* due to the fact that Jörgensen had seen Italian mysticism still alive in the area around Assisi, but had only been able to find German mysticism in books. *The Loveliest Rose* is an example of this German mysticism which Jörgensen brought to life from old manuscripts.

Strictly speaking it is not written by Jörgensen at all. Only the introduction is original, and elsewhere the author has limited himself to an adaptation of Suso's own autobiography, recapitulating it in the style of a legend, which is admirably suited to the subject. He puts the old *Book of Divine Wisdom*[17] within the reach of a modern reader. And yet this little volume is one of his most personal. The explanation of this is to be found in his ability to associate whatever he read with himself. It was his custom to underline in the works of other people sentences and passages which in some way could almost be thought of as referring to him, or reflecting the situation he was in as he read the book. In the poems he translated into Danish from other languages he succeeded in finding affinities with himself, and in many cases it is only the fact that the original poet's name is mentioned that prevents us from saying that such and such a poem is the direct result of some experience or attitude of mind which can otherwise be documented. Of course, these poems do have a direct significance; Jörgensen chose many of them simply because of their aptness in his situation. He assimilates the feelings and expressions of others. The same is true of *The*

Loveliest Rose: Jörgensen has assimilated an entire book, and without distorting Suso's *Book of Divine Wisdom,* he transforms it into a little volume which speaks clearly of himself and his own situation. Of the three great German medieval mystics, Master Eckhardt, Tauler, and Suso, the third is perhaps the least known, and thus it is again striking that it should be he Jörgensen chose to write about rather than the other two. It was obviously again a case of a kindred spirit with whose development Jörgensen felt he could identify himself.

The Loveliest Rose, with its reference to the hymn by the eighteenth-century Danish poet Brorson, in which the rose is a symbol of Christ, is not a book about a conversion, but rather about the struggle that takes place in a man after conversion. Not only does it tell of the inner struggle, but also of the persecution and suffering which become his lot because of his faith and the moral stand he adopts. Suso's struggle is told in symbolical form, but because of this it is possible to discern Jörgensen's own struggle in the background: his conversion, his struggle against sensuousness, his rejection by others and the resultant sense of isolation which later becomes even more terrible when he feels that God himself has turned away from him. In the light of Jörgensen's own troubles in the period immediately preceding, it can scarcely be a coincidence that the account of how Suso was once falsely accused ends with his prayer: "O God, what is your intention with me? O God, where is your mercy now, that mercy which they say you show your friends? Here I go waiting and waiting, and am losing my life, my possessions and my honor. . . . God has turned his beautiful eyes and his gracious face away from me!" [18]

To this he receives the reply that he must persevere until the hour of his suffering is past. The thought that his sufferings have a divine origin is his only consolation.

In one sense Suso's life forms a parallel to that of St. Francis: he has first to overcome himself, which he does by inflicting physical penances upon himself, and then he turns his religiosity outwards and seeks to save others. His principles here are stated in very similar terms to those of St. Francis: "To bring God home from exile, to open the door into the hearts of men for him was the reason why the Servant of Eternal Wisdom [i.e. Suso] traveled so far afield. And as he himself loved God with all his heart, he wished to win all men for the same heavenly love and to remove them from all selfish desires. And he succeeded with many, both men and women." [19]

This, however, was accompanied by something entirely new. For the first time there is here depicted a more introspective form of religious life, closely connected with the "cell of self-knowledge" which was to be one of the dominant themes in the book on St. Catherine. There is, in fact, a quite close connection between the two works, as Jörgensen himself has indirectly pointed out by using quotations from Suso as mottoes for the three Books into which St. Catherine is divided. The idea of the conquest of self was also present in St. Francis, but here it occupies a relatively larger space, while another theme from St. Francis, that of walking with a gulf on either side, the direct choice between good and evil, is here expressed in the idea which runs throughout the book and concerns two sorts of love, earthly and heavenly, and the need to choose between them. It was a theme Jörgensen was soon to revert to in his short portrayal of Angela of Foligno before dealing with it in more depth in St. Catherine. Both kinds of love make their demands on Suso, and he has to choose between them. He makes his choice and accepts the consequent suffering, as Jörgensen himself had done.

In the introduction, however, he tries to give the book a broader significance than a mere reflection of himself. He asks the question as to what this book about a rose really has to say to the children of the twentieth century, and answers it by arguing that even in the advanced culture of the modern age surely most people want to be flowers rather than weeds.

IV   On High (I det Höje, 1908)

While *The Loveliest Rose* was a by-product of Jörgensen's Franciscan studies, *On High* is a much more direct result of them. The relationship is most obvious in the first two parts, those dealing with Angela of Foligno and Margerita of Cortona, both of whom had previously been mentioned in *Pictures of Roman Saints*. In *On High*, however, the portrayal is more detailed, and the author shows a more thoroughly developed historical sense and is no longer bound to one single source. He writes with obvious enthusiasm and admiration, but he does not identify himself with his characters so closely as he did with St. Francis and Suso. Apart from their conversion, the lives of Angela and Margerita and Camilla Varani bear no particular similarity to that of Jörgensen, who sees this one point of contact but does not find a proper basis for identification in it. On the other hand, he does emphasize certain aspects of their conversions which resemble his own, as for instance in the passage dealing with Angela's temptations.

Far more striking in these short studies are the repeated echoes of the crisis which was developing in his own relations with his wife at this time, and of the desperate personal situation in which he found himself. At the beginning of "Angela of Foligno" he writes of her spiritual state before conversion and describes her dissatisfaction with the life she was leading:

> She was in the grip of that restlessness known to those living under conditions which they are unable to alter for the time being, but which they feel are contrary to their conscience—for instance, those living on debts, those who use more than is their due, or who allow others to do so in their name—all those who are weak and see what is right but have neither strength nor courage to do it—all those who hesitate to cut off their right hand, even though it is precisely cutting off their right hand that will open the gates of Paradise for them. . . .
> Angela was in the grip of this restlessness—of dissatisfaction with the life she was leading—and a burning desire to establish her existence in conformity with her principles, her life with her faith, her practice with her theory.[20]

Seldom did Jörgensen write anything for publication which more clearly depicted his own position at that time, his desire to put his life on a different footing, and the impossibility for him of doing so. Exactly the same situation is echoed in "Margerita of Cortona" when the writer talks of her restlessness and dissatisfaction. She is living with her lover, with whom she has a son, and the sinfulness of this manner of life becomes steadily more apparent to her. She longs to change it, but cannot:

But the years passed, and it all remained but pious wishes in Margerita's soul. She suffered under the relationship, and yet she did not break it. There was, of course, also the child to keep her bound. "But," Bossuet said, "God's Providence does not grant a respite indefinitely. It is necessary to make a decision, to bring order into your life. And those who cannot, those who can never decide, will discover one fine day that without realizing it they have reached the limit which God has laid down for their indecision." In other words, the day will come when God intervenes and says, "Thus far and no farther!"[21]

A page later there is another passage which appears to reflect domestic disturbances. Margerita's lover dies. She realizes her wrong, repents and goes home to her father. He is prepared to forgive her and receive her back into the home, but is not allowed to do so by his wife, her stepmother: "A battle took place that morning in Tancredo's home in Laviano, a battle between a kindhearted but weak man and a self-righteous, strong-willed woman, and the result was a merciless decree: 'I won't have such a wench as this in the house! Now you can choose between her and me! For I will tell you one thing—if she comes, then it is best that I should go.'"[22]

A moment of drama such as this stands out in the otherwise straightforward account of the life of a medieval saint. Suddenly the language is charged with emotion, with fury even, and this picture of the well-meaning but weak father being dominated by a hard-hearted, strong woman emerges as something which has a special significance for the author. In some strange way he seems to be writing of himself here, and this particular scene reminds us of one of the underlined passages in one of Jörgensen's books in Svendborg. The book is Sigrid Undset's *The Burning Bush*, and the passage in question is about the flirtatious Björg who, while out with some friends, has quarreled with her husband Paul by telephone. Paul goes home:

When he arrived at Otta he was told that Schijstads had gone an hour and a half ago. There was a letter for him in his room.

"I am going on to Kristiania with the Schijstads. And then I am going abroad with them. You needn't think that you can treat me just as you like. Björg."

In the margin at the side of this passage Jörgensen has written:

"Ugh! On connaît ça aussi—'Only death can stop me!' (Cologne (?) 1909)."

If the date had been 1907 instead of 1909, it might have been tempting to believe that the above passage from "Margerita of Cortona" referred to the same occasion. It can obviously not do so, but the similarity between the two is so striking that it is natural to conclude that this sort of scene was commonplace to Jörgensen. Strained relations between members of a family are mentioned in *St. Francis,* but the increasing number of such passages in works from the following years removes any doubt as to the significance of such episodes for Jörgensen himself. He is writing as much of himself as of the characters he is portraying, and the observant reader will understand the deeper meaning when he writes of Margerita: "Best of all, of course, she understood people with a nature akin to her own. . . . We often feel . . . how Margerita draws on her own experiences, and while reading her we must often admit the partial justification of Oscar Wilde's daring assertion that there is much to be learned from sin." [23]

On this basis Angela of Foligno's words of consolation also take on a new force: "And I say the same if God decrees that we should be struck by sad deaths, persecution, oppression, ignominy, attacks, and robberies. Let us not complain, but let us understand that they are all remedies prepared for us and offered to us in love by the great Doctor, our Lord and Savior, for the sake of our true welfare." [24] Such consolation was necessary to Jörgensen at this time, not only because of his difficult situation at home, but also on account of a new religious crisis which was building up, and which seems to find its expression in this very same short study of Angela of Foligno, where he talks of Angela's own religious doubts and her fear that "she might be deceiving herself, running after a phantom and a figment of the imagination, and giving away the real and tangible good things in exchange for dreams and baubles." The thought is not developed in this book, but finds its full expression in the volume of poetry Jörgensen published the following year entitled *From the Depths (Af det Dybe).* This book indicates that Jörgensen had by then passed through one of his most serious crises since his conversion.

V   St. Catherine of Siena (Den hellige Katerina af Siena, *1915*)

The mental and financial stresses which Jörgensen was undergoing at this time are reflected in the fact that it was seven
years before he published his next major work, *St. Catherine
of Siena*. The intervening years had been taken up by his journalism, much of which had been published in book form as well,
while 1913 saw the publication of *On Goethe* (*Goethe-bogen*)
and *Beyond All the Blue Mountains* (*Bag alle de blaa Bjærge*);
the latter is akin to *The Book of the Pilgrim* and is related to
St. Catherine in much the same way as the earlier work is related to *St. Francis*.

In the foreword to *St. Catherine of Siena* Jörgensen significantly remarks that she is a saint he began by fearing and ended
by loving. He felt there was about her an element of tyranny,
grounded in her indomitable will and her authority, but he
finally came under her spell in just the same way as many of
her contemporaries. This initial fear is undoubtedly the reason
why he was so long in writing the work; he began it soon after
completing *St. Francis*, but did not finish it until 1915, and thus
was actively engaged on it a longer time than on any other of
his works. Consequently, it is not the product of a single mood
or attitude of mind, for, as has been seen, he underwent various
crises both spiritual and financial during this time, and saw the
breakup of his marriage. It is therefore pointless to try to find
in it the same direct expression of a state of mind as is found
in *St. Francis*. On the other hand, in the light of the close relationship between Jörgensen and his books, and of the manner
in which he used them as a vehicle for self-expression, it is of
more than passing interest to know that in later years he considered this the best of his saints' lives.

The life of St. Catherine does not provide the same points of
contact for Jörgensen as does the biography of St. Francis.
Instead of the inner conflict caused by conversion, this portrait
is of a girl who was destined for sainthood from her very earliest
days, experiencing her first vision at the age of six, and turning
her thoughts almost exclusively to spiritual things from that day
on. Certainly, he says, her life was at first "halb' Kinderspiele,
halb' Gott im Herzen," but her delight in playing at the religious

life of a hermit gradually led to a more serious attraction to it. After refusing to marry at the wish of her parents, she was allowed to live a secluded life in her own home, and extraordinarily was permitted to become a member of the Dominican Third Order, the Mantellate. During all this time she was subject to visions and mystical experiences, culminating in her mystical betrothal to Christ in 1367.

This completes the first Book, "Solitude," while the second, "The Imitation of Christ," is concerned with Catherine's return to a more active life, first in her own home, later in the world at large. In this, and particularly in her completely unselfish care of the poor and sick, even when they had wronged her, she clearly reminds us of St. Francis. The difference, however, lies in the fact that his life of activity in the world came relatively early and gradually led to the contemplative final years, while her early years of contemplation served as the prelude to activities on a larger scale. She first turned her attention to persuading the Pope to return from Avignon to Italy, and she succeeded, though she was less successful in her efforts to bring about a new crusade. Throughout all this her mystical experiences and ecstasies continued and became even more intense, and while the first Book ends with the mystical betrothal, the second closes with the account of St. Catherine's stigmatization.

Book Three, "The Crown of Thorns," which occupies half the entire work, begins with what amounts to a triumphal introduction concerned with Catherine's theocratic views and a general exposition of her philosophy. It goes on to tell of her political activities in the last five years of her life, her constant work on behalf of the Pope, and her efforts to mediate between him and his numerous enemies in the strife-torn Italy of the fourteenth century and in face of the Great Schism. Much of this Book is devoted to a statement of Catherine's thought, in particular as expressed in her book *Il Dialogo*, and to her final spiritual testament, closing, not with her death in 1380, but with the scene in Siena when her head was brought in solemn procession back to her home town as a sacred relic. A life of dedication and determination is thus brought to a fittingly triumphal conclusion.

Clearly, there is little here comparable with Jörgensen's own life, and a possible affinity must be sought elsewhere. It seems

likely that the point of contact between Catherine and him is
to be found less in her career or manner of life than in her
philosophy, in certain basic thoughts to which he returns again
and again. Quite early in the book, on page 31 in the second
Danish edition, he makes his first reference to her idea of a
choice that has to be made between two ways of life; although
it is never explicitly stated, it is the choice which Jörgensen
himself had been faced with, and, indeed, to judge from all
available evidence, still was faced with while he was writing
this book. It may well be her stubborn insistence on the inevi-
tability of this choice which made St. Catherine seem frighten-
ing to Jörgensen in the early part of his work on her—it was a
choice which he would at times have liked to avoid, but which
she emphasizes quite uncompromisingly. Thus, at the beginning
of Chapter VI, Jörgensen recounts one of her visions in which
she sees a tree full of magnificent fruit, but difficult of access
because of a thick hedge. Nearby was a corn field, but the ears
were barren and turned to dust if touched. Some passers-by
looked at the fruit of the tree, but were put off by the hedge,
and turned their attention instead to the corn, which turned to
dust and robbed them of their strength. Others managed to get
through the hedge, but were then alarmed at how high the
fruit hung on the tree, and went in their turn to the corn field.
Yet others persisted and plucked the fruit and ate it and were
spiritually strengthened by it and would thereafter never eat
anything else: "This early vision contains the whole essence of
Catherine's view of life as it was to be developed in richer and
more profound form in the following years. Man, she feels, is
placed between two powers, both of which are seeking his favor.
One of these powers is love, life, peace, happiness, and bliss—
the other is outward appearance, the world, satanic delusion,
which always bewitches and always ends in disappointment." [25]
     This is Jörgensen's interpretation of the vision, and he goes
on to point out that the idea of a choice belongs not only to
St. Catherine but to apostolic Christianity. He follows it through
St. Augustine's conception of the two cities to the idea of the
two sorts of love expressed in Dominican mysticism (and which
he himself had treated in *The Loveliest Rose*) and to Ignatius
of Loyola's conceit of the two banners. Thus, at a very early

stage he puts St. Catherine firmly in the Christian tradition and especially relates her to the question of choice which has preoccupied him in his earlier work.

Fifty pages later he returns to the theme and develops it:

> There are two sorts of love in Man—love of God and one's neighbor, and love of the world. There are two sorts of will in Man—the will of God and the selfish will of Man himself. One of those two powers—love of the world, selfish will—leads to inner conflict, sin, misfortune, all kinds of evil and eternal damnation. The other—love of God and of one's neighbor—leads to inner peace, spiritual well-being, all kinds of virtue and eternal life.
>
> This is the great realization which is the basis of all Catherine's thought and existence. From pure egoism we must take off our own selfish will and clothe ourselves in God's will—for the world which we long to own passes, life is as a fragile glass, or like running water which disappears beneath a bridge—*tutto passa*.[26]

Because of the personal element in Jörgensen's work, it is natural to ask here whether his interpretation of Catherine's thought reflects something of his own state of mind as well as personal knowledge of the effects of worldliness and a sense of his need to turn his back on this—for purely selfish reasons. Perhaps there is also the suggestion of conflict caused by the intellectual acknowledgment of the necessity of doing this, as well as the emotional reaction against it. In *The Book of the Pilgrim* he had earlier pointed out that the original conflict for him had been between feeling and intellect. The spiritual peace he here refers to is also alluded to in *St. Catherine* with a quotation from St. Augustine: "Our hearts are restless until they find rest in you, O God."

This preoccupation with choice and the results of Man's choice continues throughout the book, with the increasing sense of the passing of time implied by *tutto passa*. (Jörgensen's letters indicate that he himself had a marked sense of the passage of time.) Later (p. 148) the choice is given as two types of water, both inviting us to drink them. Yet another instance of choice is put in political terms, perhaps as a result of the First World War, which was being fought as Jörgensen wrote the book.

In his subsequent exposition of Catherine's philosophy Jörgensen naturally returns to the idea of choice, and spends some considerable time on it:

> The essence of the soul—Catherine teaches—is *amor,* love or will. The will can go in two directions—outwards or inwards. Outwards the will acts from love of creation, of the world, of the flesh—that is "die falsche Minne," as Suso said, selfishness, pleasure-loving egoism. Inwards the will acts from love of God and one's neighbor, in self-abnegation, self-denial, and this is the true love, that which in truth deserves this name. These two directions of the will lead by two different routes to two contrasting worlds—egoism to tension, darkness, passion, constant disturbance and unrest and impatience—in other words it leads to hell. While the fruits of true love are peace, light, joy—that is to say: heaven.[27]

There is a striking uniformity in the construction of these various passages, and the choice is always listed as the same one. Consequently, the idea of choice becomes a constantly recurring leitmotiv in the book, and predominates more, for instance, than is the case in Sigrid Undset's book on the saint. Choice, as well as the perspective it affords, is of compulsive power in Jörgensen's book, as essential to it as the portrayal of Catherine's work and achievement, and to the author it appears to be one of the two outstanding personal links with his work. It is, exceptionally, a link of personal preoccupation rather than direct affinity.

The other link, however, is more traditional, the same as one of Jörgensen's affinities with St. Francis—his knowledge that Catherine was also a poet. Indeed, on one occasion he directly refers to this similarity when remarking that St. Catherine, like St. Francis, was a traveling singer of God.[28]

Jörgensen was always fascinated by the problem of poetic inspiration, often remarking in his diaries that he had been writing as though his pen had been guided for him, or as if he personally had not been in control of what he said. In St. Catherine he also finds inspiration, religious inspiration rather than poetic, but he finds an affinity there, and links her written inspiration with her visions. Again, the nature of visions and of mystical experience is a problem to which he returns on many occasions in his works. Visions, mysticism, inspiration, both religious and poetical, seem for him to be varied facets of a whole, and they are early put into relationship with Christianity, which in Chapter III is referred to as "a religion of visions and revelations." On that same page Jörgensen refers to Catherine as a visionary, like St. Bridget of Sweden (this is of significance when we look for unity in his work), and embarks upon a discussion of inspiration, which, he says, always has something about it which is reminiscent of what visionaries tell of their sensations: "The poet or artist intensely engaged in his work feels himself raised above normal physical demands, completely dedicated to his work, and this work progresses easily, without hindrance or inhibition, as though a foreign power, another personality, was the real source of production. 'I am but an instrument, the Master plays me,' one Danish poet has said." [29]

After quoting Nietzsche on inspiration, he continues: "The ecstasy in which a St. Bridget and a St. Catherine have their religious visions and receive their revelations is a further development of that poetic inspiration." [30] Catherine is then presented as a poetical mind which reached maturity at an early age, "a religious genius in a body completely dominated by the spirit." While the essence of a mere poetical genius is communion with humanity, he says, the essence of a religious genius is communion with God.

Having made this statement and this distinction, Jörgensen is nonetheless noticeably preoccupied with St. Catherine's poetical gifts. He talks of her literary powers and also, with considerable significance for an understanding of his own attitude to his work, of her intuitive understanding:

Catherine's giftedness . . . was purely intuitive—she understood without being able to say why she understood. All poetry, all psychological art, is based on this intuitive sharp-sightedness, this ability to see into the depths and to see the truth, which might well be accompanied by a striking lack of ability to form or follow a logical argument. A great poet is seldom a profound thinker—which does not prevent the poet from understanding what is hidden to the thinker. We also find intuitive genius in great inventors and discoverers, often accompanied by weak logical abilities. And many will know how a foreign language which they only partially command can at important moments become clear and familiar to them—even to such an extent that it afterwards seems to them that they were spoken to in their own language.[31]

There is an obvious attempt here to penetrate the nature of a gift which Jörgensen knew himself to have, an intuitive understanding of a situation or a personality, though surprisingly enough he does not demonstrate this ability as brilliantly in *St. Catherine* as in *St. Francis*. On the other hand, he makes a lengthy and serious analysis of her poetic style. Starting from the comparison he makes between her and St. Francis, he introduces his analysis by talking of her gifts in general: "In particular she possessed the essential quality of a poet—the ability to create a perfect metaphor, the simile which, like a chemical or mathematical formula and at the same time in a completely tangible and visible manner, says just what he wants to say, straying neither to the left nor to the right of what is correct." [32]

Then follows a lengthy review of Catherine's metaphors and similes, with comments on the suitability of many of them, and a brief review of her use of biblical language and expression. Other expressions remind Jörgensen of the Fathers of the Church, and he finishes his review of possible literary antecedents by wondering whether she knew Dante. There is no direct reference to him in her work, but odd phrases are reminiscent of him. However, he continues, Catherine was a poet in her own right, and he lists examples from her work which exemplify her own creative ability: the ravens screeching *cras, cras*—tomorrow, tomorrow—and her vision of the keys of heaven, rusted by sin, being made bright and shining by the blood of Christ. From this brief description of her manner of writing, there is a natural transition to the statement of what she says, her philosophy, to which reference has already been made. There can, surely, be few hagiographies which include a lengthy analysis of the saint's work from a literary point of view together with an examination, albeit a tentative one, of the nature of religious inspiration. Like Catherine, Jörgensen is a poet in his own right, and he now gives much fuller rein to his literary abilities than had previously been the case. He is now quite conscious of this aspect of his work and uses it as the basis for an analysis of a rather unusual aspect of the saint, thus raising his biography to a completely different level from that of conventional hagiography.

Jörgensen's own poetical gifts assert themselves here in much the same way as in *St. Francis,* though perhaps with greater frequency and at times in a somewhat bolder form which foreshadows some of the techniques which were later to be adopted. In particular, he makes a partial return to the descriptions of nature at which he had previously excelled, and he starts on a more directly personal approach which is to become so striking a feature of his later work. Thus, the introduction, like that of *St. Francis,* is partly fictional. Starting from the historically accurate account of Catherine's first vision at the age of six, he embellishes the bare historical fact and paints a realistic picture of two children coming home along the streets of Siena. Not content with this, however, he puts himself directly into the picture and starts his second paragraph with: "And one evening in the year 1912 I, a stranger, walk through Siena and endeavor as far as possible to trace the steps of those two children, which have been submerged by the traffic of almost six centuries." And the next paragraph: "So I imagine those two children walking hand in hand through the darkening streets of Siena. Perhaps they say nothing to each other—it often happens that children walk along together without saying a word. But they are thinking, and I will try to follow their thoughts." [33]

This opening technique is essentially the same as that of *St. Francis,* though the uninhibited intrusion of Jörgensen speaking in the first person is new, and adds a new element of intimacy to his work. Fittingly, the book ends on the same note, or a development of it. Again a historical fact is embellished by the modern writer. The bare fact that St. Catherine's head was borne in solemn procession through the streets of Siena is developed into a fictional description of the procession itself in all its pomp and splendor: the children, the guilds, the hermits who have come from outside the city "with long beards, serious, barefoot, in clothes of camel hair," the monks of various orders, and the clergy, first the priests, then the abbots, then the bishops, and finally the sacred relic under a canopy. During this description Jörgensen has imperceptibly changed from the past to the present tense. This not unusual literary technique is, however, further exploited as the climax of the scene approaches, and from being merely a literary trick to heighten the dramatic effect of a scene, the present tense comes really to represent the present, and the remaining page is written as though Jörgensen himself is really on the spot, describing what is taking place:

All the bells are ringing as though in ecstasy, they chatter and shout and rejoice in one confused chorus with their tiny silver voices. . . . And listen! Now *il Campanone* starts—how it resounds and thunders —it is as though someone were striking the very vault of heaven. . . . *Il Campanone* is ringing—and we all begin to weep. . . .

But there, behind the canopy, just behind those who are carrying the reliquary, first among the Mantellate with their white robes and black cloaks—the little, frail old woman who is almost bent double— her withered hands are folded with such piety—her eyes stare up at the gold and brilliance before her—the thin, violet lips move in prayer—the tears run without ceasing from the red eyes down over the wrinkled cheeks. . . .

But of course, it is Lapa. Catherine's mother, almost ninety years of age. She it is—there she goes before us, she herself, she who gave birth to the saint. Happy Lapa! And we are all on our knees—and we are all weeping—and with eyes blinded by tears we see the canopy pass—and the candles—and the incense—and the bishop— and Raimund—and Lapa—blessed Lapa—*Lapa beata.* Lapa, blessed among women, and blessed is the fruit of thy womb, Catherine.[34]

Technically this is a masterly finish to the book, bringing it up to the present in its message and urgency, and the echo of the Hail Mary in the last line adds final emphasis to the con- temporaneity of Catherine's significance. The transition from past to fictional present to real present is a simple one externally, but the effect is to add a new perspective to what has gone before.

Jörgensen has, however, spoken in the first person on various occasions in the work, and he has also on one occasion made earlier use of apostrophe to Catherine's mother Lapa; it occurs in the early part of the book when Lapa has discovered Cather- ine practising flagellation and is overcome with emotion: "*Sem- plicissima Lapa*— you loved your little Catherine so much, the child of your heart, the last of your children, whom you had suckled yourself, the sunlight in your house, the beautiful little

Euphrosyne—and now you could not understand why she should commit violence upon herself . . . we feel for you, we understand you, we love you." [35]

This sudden, direct, emotional outburst in a work of scholarship has a most striking effect; it draws the reader's attention to an otherwise unexpected aspect of the story of St. Catherine, depicting Lapa as a woman suffering mental anguish through the religious zeal of her daughter. Lapa's role throughout is one of opposition changing through reserve into discipleship, and the final glimpse of her in tears combines the glory of triumphant saintliness with a mother's loss. Her role is in fact a shadowy reflection of that of Mary, surrendering her will to that of Christ, suffering through it and yet accepting, and finally seen at the foot of the Cross. This parallel is enhanced and completed by the mystical betrothal of Catherine to Christ. Thus Lapa herself comes to represent that self-abnegation which Catherine preaches, and so is closely connected with the idea of choice on which the book is based.

The parallel between Lapa and Mary exists, but it has not to any significant extent affected the portrayal of Lapa as an Italian mother. On the contrary, Jörgensen has obviously drawn on his knowledge of the Italians and their manner of speaking in order to portray her, and the result is a series of vivid but brief glimpses of family life. Lapa cannot at the beginning of the book understand Catherine's aversion to men, and comments: "Good heavens, they aren't poisonous!" [36] To this Jörgensen adds that Catherine avoided them as though they were serpents. The way in which he has treated this minute scene becomes obvious if it is compared with Sigrid Undset's account of it; she merely comments: "She even shunned the apprentices and journeymen in the home 'as though they were serpents'".[37] Both accounts are taken directly from Raymond of Capua's contemporary biography of St. Catherine, which in the English translation has: "Whenever the apprentices in her father's dye works, who lived with the family, came near her, she would rush off as though there were serpents after her—much to everyone's amazement." [38] As will be seen from these quotations, Sigrid Undset has taken Raymond of Capua's version almost word for word, but Jörgensen has adapted it, given it dramatic content by changing an indirect report into a scene with direct speech in which Lapa expresses her feelings in the language of everyday life. This is no isolated instance, but is rather the pattern for Jörgensen's treatment of Raymond's text wherever this is possible. The reader is constantly aware of Jörgensen's personal knowledge and experience interpreting the original account.

Similarly, he uses this personal knowledge to illustrate and support in a more external manner. Catherine's mystical betrothal in 1367 takes place on Shrove Tuesday, Carnival Day, and Jörgensen uses his knowledge of the carnival season in Siena to portray the background of that day, creating, incidentally, a new dramatic effect by the violent contrast between Catherine's mystical experience and the worldly gaiety by which it is surrounded. He also uses his knowledge of the countryside around Siena to fill in the background, and this gives him an opportunity for a return to a limited and purified form of nature description. No longer is nature personified, but instead it is described in measured, almost objective terms, which nevertheless on occasion produce descriptions of great beauty:

The countryside between Asciano and Mont' Oliveto Maggiore looks today just as it did at the time of Francesco Malavolti and Neri de' Pagliaresi. It is what is known as the *Creta*—a peculiar desert landscape consisting of nothing but barren hills furrowed by heavy rain, cracked by the sun, across which the road winds wearily up from Asciano to the little town of Chiusure and to the huge old monastery. Round Asciano the valley is still green with corn and vines or—in May—clad in the red carpet of clover. But you are soon up among the ashen gray hills—they are like dunes—but they are of clay, not sand, and they look as though they were upholstered with wrinkled elephant hide. The waves of clay become more and more bare, sharper and sharper on the ridges; the wind blows cold, the plateaus are desolate, with only a lonely farmstead with a few cypresses and a little thin corn in the fields which have been cultivated with such great labor. Before you tower Mont' Amiata, Monte Cetona, Montepulciano, and if you turn back you see far away on the blue horizon Siena like a shining vision, and despite the distance of sixteen miles you can glimpse the bell tower of the Cathedral and the *Torre del Mangia* of the Town Hall.[39]

It is a chastened form of nature description, with references to the labor of the peasant and with religious overtones in the references to the monastery and the Cathedral. It is intimately connected with the narrative, here concerned with a journey on foot during Lent, and is followed by a direct personal reminiscence by Jörgensen which in its turn also leads to a further understanding of the two travelers. It is admittedly surmising, but it belongs to that category of intuitive interpretation to which reference has already been made. Elsewhere there are other descriptions of a similar sort, one even telling how the countryside makes people long to wander out into it, and this is further developed to explain Catherine's actions—though elsewhere Jörgensen says that she seems to have had very little feeling for nature.

It is more difficult in *St. Catherine* than is usual in Jörgensen's work to assess how much he includes of his own experience. There are certainly personal echoes, most probably in the scenes of domestic strife. Similarly, it is evident that there are elements of a literary self-portrait—in Stefano Maconi who defies his family in order to follow Catherine, in Neri, the poet turned disciple, and in the English hermit, William Flete, who admires her but lacks the strength to follow her. The presence of Andrée Carof as a main source of inspiration is apparent in almost everything Jörgensen wrote from the time he met her until her death in 1933, and it seems likely that she has had some influence on the depiction of Catherine. She herself was something of a Catherine, and it is quite conceivable that Jörgensen's changed attitude to Catherine is in some measure the result of his meeting with her. It is certainly beyond doubt that the portrayal of Stefano Maconi and his devotion to Catherine reflects something of Jörgensen's feelings for Andrée Carof, while the opposition of Stefano's family echoes the opposition Jörgensen himself had experienced.

But no matter how much influence Andrée Carof may have had on the final shape of the book, her most far-reaching effect on it was doubtless the fact that she more than anyone finally reconciled Jörgensen to his new faith and strengthened him in his religious beliefs. In this way she also reconciled him to St. Catherine and made it possible for him to feel not only awe but also affection for the figure he was portraying. Thus, both outwardly and inwardly *St. Catherine of Siena* comes to represent the essential transition in Jörgensen's life, the movement away from the spiritual and domestic chaos which he had been experiencing for years. It is little wonder that he loved this book more than his other biographies.

CHAPTER 4

The Travel Books

IT is not being unfair to Jörgensen's later works to argue that the most important part of his output lies in the years up to the publication of his autobiography, *The Legend of My Life*. In the twenty years or so from the time immediately preceding his conversion and up to 1917, when the *Legend* began to appear, Jörgensen wrote with a power and concentration which was not to return, except, perhaps in the case of *Charles de Foucauld*, when the special circumstances in which this book was written restored Jörgensen's former power. This early concentration and urgency, found in the poetry as well as in the prose, was doubtless a result of the conflict in Jörgensen's own mind at the time, and the lack of drama in much of his later work can likewise be seen as the result of comparative peace of mind for long periods.

Throughout his life as an author Jörgensen wrote travel books, some of them mere collections of newspaper articles with few literary pretensions, but others true works of art in their own right. The best ones are intimately related to Jörgensen's main work and belong in general to the period of his major hagiographies; and therefore, it will be natural to examine them in conjunction with the works with which they are most closely associated.

I The Book of Travel (Rejsebogen, 1895)

The Book of Travel immediately strikes the reader as Jörgensen's first really Catholic work, despite the fact that it was written before his actual reception into the Church. At all events, he openly stands here as a Christian apologist, for which reason his French translator, Téodor de Wyzewa, called the book "une audacieuse apologie des dogmes, du culte et de l'esprit catholiques." There is much to be said for considering *The Book of Travel* as one of his Catholic works: its content is typical of the later travel accounts with their characteristic mixture of pure description of travel, lyricism, memoirs, philosophical musings, polemics, and Catholic information all of which is worked into a complicated arabesque. Stylistically the book is partly inspired by the medieval legend, but, like later works, contains few emotive adjectives and relies on simple description with little recourse to personification of nature. The writer still loves nature as much as ever, though perhaps with a twinge of conscience now that it must be seen no longer as the source of mysterious powers, but as a mirror of God's glory.

In spite of this, *The Book of Travel* is a natural continuation of the early novels, providing a further treatment of the same problems and still arriving at no firm conclusion. The struggle between an atheistic, pantheistic view of life and Christian faith, which was apparent in the last two novels, is a dominant theme here. On the one hand, the reader is aware of the poet's desire to accept a Catholic view of life, symbolized by his visit to the monastery of Beuron, his presence in Portiuncula to witness the scene on the first day of August when people streamed into the tiny church to obtain a plenary indulgence, and by his journey to Montefalco to visit the shrine of St. Clara of Montefalco. On the other hand, he flees from Beuron and returns to nature and the life of the ordinary people nearby, and despite his emotion at Portiuncula and an understanding of the significance of the scene he has just witnessed, he writes expressly in the following chapter: "And yet he did not believe . . .," and closes it with a nature description expressing the sense of distance which is so characteristic of many of the more emotional passages in the novels: "And Giovanni sat and listened to [the two voices], while he looked out over the Umbrian plain where only a solitary light was lit, far away near Santa Maria degli Angeli. A dog barked far away in the distance. And down in the street the old fountain splashed and splashed." [1]

Jörgensen's reaction after his visit to the shrine of St. Clara is more violent, more direct, and he denotes as a lie the explanation given him by a Professor Pennacchi of the three stones which were found in her heart; the professor contended that they should be seen as a symbol of the Trinity, each weighing the same, but all together weighing the same as one. This is understandably too much for the poet, his feelings get the better of him, and he feels a complete outsider. On their way home his companions are portrayed as pious Catholics, saying their rosaries, but Jörgensen feels the call of his old pantheistic self: "And when they were finally in the carriage again and evening was sinking over the endless plain, Giovanni sat as among strangers. The rosaries were taken out, and even the coachman took part in the prayer. But Giovanni merely sat and looked at the moon, rising large and red behind the mountains, and he wished himself far away." [2] The moon is the same as in *Summer*, the symbol of nature's magical power, and Jörgensen experiences the same longing away from reality that was one of the features of *Spring Legend*. This chapter is followed by one showing his break with Catholicism, as a direct result of which he returns home, as he has often longed to do. But he immediately begins to long for Italy.

Apart from these indisputable signs of personal conflict the book contains another characteristic of Jörgensen's later work. Aware of the fact that his countrymen do not know very much about Catholicism, he undertakes the role of an educator, explaining monastic life, defending indulgences, describing the Mass, and trying to give an impression of the daily life of a devout Catholic. By way of contrast he indulges in a short polemical attack on the "modern" way of life in Denmark. These instructive passages are plain to see, though they do not dominate the work. They are of a type which appears in varying degrees in practically all Jörgensen's later work, especially, of course, the travel descriptions and essays, but also in the hagiography, where they normally emerge as a result of reflections on some aspect of the account.

II   The Book of the Pilgrim (Pilgrimsbogen, 1903)

Such didactic passages also occur in the next "travel account," *The Book of the Pilgrim* (English translation: *Pilgrim Walks in Franciscan Italy*, 1908), but they are of less significance in this book, one of the most personal and beautiful Jörgensen ever wrote. The author himself is the central feature; everything is experienced directly through his eyes and with his feelings. He does not feel committed to any narrowly defined subject, but wanders from topic to topic, indulging freely in the digressions which were so dear to his heart. However, the present concern is more with the subjective experience of what he sees and encounters than with the outward aspects of his journeys in Franciscan Italy, and he describes with profound personal feeling the way in which he became acquainted with and was moved by the Franciscan way of life. His intuitive gifts, which had already been just discernible in his early attempts at hagiography, are allowed free play, and thus his lyrical and apologetic powers are fused in a work which stands as one of the major achievements of his early Catholic period.

It is quite obvious from the very beginning that he has overcome his doubts about his being justified in continuing as a writer, and along with his deepening understanding of Franciscan life goes the change from lingering doubt to faith. This process covers more than half the book, beginning with the description of the countryside around the monastery of La Foresta. The poet is possessed by the ardent love of the Italian countryside, and this forces him to think of his future call in life:

Ah, Italy, my Italy. Italy—thus do I see you, feel you, love you! Shall I ever succeed in bringing my countrymen at home in Denmark to appreciate you, to love you and to understand you, as I understand and love you? Germany has long been a part of our cultural life, while France and England came later. But is there room for Italy, for the real, true, profound, genuine and simple Italy, the Italy which in Fonte Columba I called Franciscan Italy? *Have* I a task in life? And does this task consist in acquainting people with that Italy? Or is all I do of no avail? . . . Who has not known such hours when we are about to lose our faith in what is deepest down within us, the essence of our life, the justification for our existence? Those are the moments when in his heart of hearts the poet doubts the truth of everything he proclaims in his work.[3]

The religious doubts which are indicated in this last sentence seem concerned not with dogma but rather with the cultural significance of Catholicism. Jörgensen gives the impression that he was influenced by the argument that Catholicism is inimical to progress and that the northern, Protestant cultures are superior. Perhaps it was simply a question of how far he was justified in preaching the simple, medieval Franciscan ideal to the patently progressive, modern civilization in Denmark. Meanwhile his doubts are stilled by Padre Angelo, whom he meets unexpectedly and to whom he opens his heart. The priest's reply deals merely with the religious question and is in fact a defense of the attitude of the Church, much the same as Jörgensen's own defense in his earlier work. The problem of the poet's duty in life appears not to be mentioned, but as it was this question which gave rise to the entire passage, it is natural to conclude that Padre Angelo also persuaded him to continue writing. At this period of his life the question of a vocation was essential to Jörgensen, and it is unlikely that the removal of secondary doubts would entirely have set his mind at rest.

He does not return to this problem of vocation, and when he later refers to Angela of Foligno's feeling of being incapable of expressing her profoundest religious experiences, and repeats her cry: "Brother, I am blaspheming, I am blaspheming!" he goes on to give her words general significance: "Is that not what everyone must say, everyone who from within his own poor self dares to write of the most sublime things, and then sees people reaching for his words in order to find light, wisdom, guidance?" [4] There are still doubts as to his own ability, but he implies that he has no longer any doubts about using his pen.

Another sign of the removal of hesitation is to be seen later in the book in connection with Jörgensen's conjecture that occasionally one of St. Francis' followers might have had his doubts and felt "that everything was madness, and that the best thing for him was to go back to the city. . . . Yes, there must indeed have been such moments when more than one of these 'penitents from Assisi,' as they originally called themselves, felt his ardor for penitence weaken." [5] It has been suggested[6] that this remark indicates the persistence of Jörgensen's own religious doubt, but it is surely rather a doubt as to the result of what he is undertaking. It is not faith which weakens, but the ardor for penitence, that is to say, the way in which the Franciscans implement their faith, and which corresponds to Jörgensen's loss of confidence in his own books and in the effect they are having. This interpretation is also indicated by the final resolution of the problem. After telling how one of the brothers does in fact lapse, Jörgensen goes on: "But all the others persevered—they persevered and won. . . . They persevered as Carlyle persevered many centuries later when he sat writing his completely unpopular books, the books which brought him nothing but shame, scorn, and constantly increasing poverty. . . . Until the day came when his books had educated a new generation, and a regenerated England greeted him as its teacher, savior, benefactor, and guide." [7]

This is the point of the entire passage. Taken as a whole it indicates not doubt, but confidence, even complete faith in the ultimate significance of his books. Jörgensen had undertaken a task which he had previously compared with that of Carlyle, and here he realizes that he might have a long wait before his activities finally bear fruit, but he feels that they will do so in the end. The final solution to all these questions is indicated at the end of the book, after the author's last conversation with Father Samuel, who has read him St. Francis' farewell to La Verna and discussed its significance: "That second night I slept peacefully in La Verna. What I had seen that day, and what Father Samuel had told me, had, as it were, opened doors deep down within me—doors through which light shone, and which I instinctively knew led to the daylight, life, and happiness." [8] All doubt has disappeared, and it is fitting that the writer should have chosen to finish the book with this theme which, together with an increasing sense of intimacy with Franciscan life, has been so essential to it.

With the profound love of nature that was his, Jörgensen could scarcely help loving St. Francis and his followers. "Yes," says one of the monks in the book, "when all is said and done, nature is and always will be the best place to worship God, to worship, praise, and glorify the creator of all things, the good father of all living creatures." [9] There is no great conflict between Jörgensen's earlier pantheism and these words, or perhaps it would be better to say that this type of Christian approach would be bound to appeal to him with the attitude he had once had. However, there is nothing pantheistic about this view of nature as expressed by the Franciscan monk or by Jörgensen himself, and it would be completely wrong to imagine that he continued his pantheistic fantasies under the cloak of Franciscanism. It is rather that the deep love of nature which had quite naturally led the seeking freethinker to pantheism, made the newly converted Catholic receptive to that delight in nature, so prevalent among the Franciscans, which he came in contact with during this journey. There were other qualities in St. Francis and his followers, especially their ethical views, which would have appealed to him in any case; their attitude to nature was merely a more immediate point of contact.

And it is precisely the Franciscan *delight* which is stressed in *The Book of the Pilgrim,* the delight in nature, in life, and in everything which God has created. And the writer's obvious insistence on this is his reaction to the unhappy time which had preceded his own conversion, when he was concerned only with himself and his endless problems. Now his melancholy is replaced by joy, light, and life, words which constantly recur like leitmotivs. It is the joy, he says in one passage, "in being in *truth and love,*" while elsewhere when talking of reverence for all the real values of existence he sees this reverence for life and the good powers of life to be a truly ethical spirit. In the final analysis it was this aspect of Franciscanism which was most important to him.

He sees this spirit as something originally belonging to the Middle Ages. During Jörgensen's visit to Greccio the reader is afforded a powerful impression of a vanished age. Even the description of the monastery's location, high up on the slope of a mountain, reminds us of one of Dürer's landscapes with a castle on a rocky mountainside, apparently inaccessible and far from the bustle of the outside world. Here, in Greccio, Jörgensen himself experienced the Middle Ages: "I think I have experienced a considerable number of unusual and moving things in my life—but I can scarcely think of anything more moving than those minutes of silence among the Franciscans in Greccio. Among these barefooted men in their brown cowls, praying there in the darkness with hands uplifted, I had the most powerful feeling ever granted to me of what the Middle Ages really were." [10]

And subsequently stressing the heroic and epic aspects of the Franciscan movement, he compares this heroic form of medieval Christianity with that of the twentieth century: "I will not deny that our modern form of religion is a form of Christianity. . . . We modern Christians do not understand much of many aspects of it; we appreciate the beauty in the lives of the ancient hermits, but we have not the strength to follow their examples." [11]

The Middle Ages are for Jörgensen the culmination of Christianity and of civilization as a whole, and therefore he stresses the virtues of that age at every opportunity. In *Pictures of Roman Saints* he had emphasized the unity of medieval Catholic Europe, and here he goes further and draws his reader's attention to the ways in which the medieval times were supreme from a religious point of view. The religious ideas were different then; now, argues Jörgensen, Christianity is social rather than individual, but then personal sanctity was the aim. This is why visions and revelations were so common in the Middle Ages and so rare now, for nowadays few people attain to such sanctity. Jörgensen's praise of personal holiness may here indicate a slight shift in emphasis even at this early stage, a slight movement away from his preoccupation with the social responsibilities of Christianity. There is, however, no contradiction, as the two aspects exist side by side, but reflections such as these may well be an early sign of the interest in mysticism and personal piety which was to come later.

The most striking characteristic of *The Book of the Pilgrim* is the intense personal warmth with which it is written. This is stressed by the presence of a number of qualities previously seen in the novels and the poems. Mood plays a dominant part in this book, and the various moods are brought out largely by sense impressions of a sort which had been missing in Jörgensen's more recent work. The tone is set right at the beginning when the poet talks of his longing for the Sabine mountains and "the places and cities, the towns and valleys, the lonely monasteries, and the even lonelier mountains which it was my intention to visit." In other words, *The Book of the Pilgrim* describes the fulfilment of a longing, and the emotive aspects are made apparent from the very first page. Time after time the

writer surrenders himself to his mood, as for instance when making the ascent to the lonely monastery of Greccio. The sense of distance and the sound impressions which are both characteristic and significant in Jörgensen's work, assert themselves when his feelings get the better of him: "It is quite still around me, still as it can only be out in the country. The odd sounds in the distance can be heard so clearly: a man shuts a door in a house on the other side of the valley, and it is as though it were happening only ten steps away from me." [12] He hears a song he recognizes, and this, together with the impressions of nature, conjures up a memory: "Overpowered by memory I sat down by the wayside. It was an entire past age which came back to me, sweet and painful like everything that has vanished in the past. It was the memory of my second youth which came to me, of that beautiful summer almost ten years ago in the mountainous solitude of La Rocca under Padre Felice's roof, and with my friend Francesco by my side." [13]

Two days later, when he is distressed because of his approaching departure from Greccio, he stands by the window and looks out over the darkened landscape: "There are no stars; all is black; only in the far distance can I see a powerful glow over Rieti with its electric light. The frogs are croaking, quietly and incessantly." [14] It could almost be taken from *Summer*. Examples such as these are constantly appearing in this book, in which mood often dominates a scene when the author's feelings take possession of him. *The Book of the Pilgrim* is like one great prose poem in which the poet feels at liberty to express himself through his feelings rather than his intellect. He tried the same manner of writing in later works, but nowhere with the same perfect unity which he achieved here.

III   Beyond All the Blue Mountains
(Bag alle de blaa Bjærge, *1913*)

The Book of the Pilgrim serves as an introduction to *St. Francis*, and a similar relationship exists between *Beyond All the Blue Mountains* and *St. Catherine*. Jörgensen tells in rhapsodic language of a period he spent in Siena and the surrounding countryside, while the blue mountains he can see from his

window come to symbolize his longing. It is a restless work—
in this respect very different from *The Book of the Pilgrim*—
bearing obvious traces of the strains and stresses the author
was experiencing during its composition. There were strained
relations with his wife, renewed doubts as to the value of his
activities, perhaps religious doubts, a sense of both physical and
spiritual homelessness which made him feel "merely an ill-
defined desire to be on the move and to see far away, look at
the vast landscape which stretches from the gates of Siena to the
blue mountains." [15] Later, in a passage in which he describes
the landscape in terms foreshadowing the nature description of
St. Catherine, the same symbol returns: "That is where I want
to go, out into the spreading, green countryside, out towards
the mountains which appear blue in the haze." As he himself
points out when he hears some German nuns singing a German
hymn and thereby comes to long for Denmark, this is basically
a case of *Dort, wo du nicht bist*, even if his restlessness can be
easily explained. It is presumably this feeling, too, which fills
him with disgust with himself and makes him feel like an "old,
homeless bird" which can do nothing but sing "Do not forget"
and "Alas in times past." It would be difficult to find any other
book in which Jörgensen wrote so disparagingly about himself,
and in fact it is as though in the course of the book he has
sensed the dangers to himself of this new attitude. At all events,
in the final section, when he describes a stay in Belgrade, he
tells of his surprise at the friendly reception he was given
merely because he was Danish. In general terms he comments
that the evil things the Danes say of each other at home do not
appear to penetrate beyond the frontier and harm them in other
people's eyes. Here the tone suddenly changes, and although he
apparently goes on writing of the Danes as a whole, his next
words can only apply to himself, and they can only be fully understood against the background of the strange disgust with
himself which he has previously expressed:

Nevertheless, we had probably better be careful not to go too far
in the sport of self-degradation—for the moment will come when you
yourself will believe you are a good-for-nothing.—And that will be
the end of your desire to work and ability to work. Even if we do

think that others see more in us than is justifiable, then for Heaven's
sake let them do so. It spurs us on to *become* what they already
believe we are; it gives us the courage and assurance to do honor to
our name and banner. Better to stumble, to fall, and then to rise up
again than to be submerged in hopeless and powerless self-condemnation.[16]

The self-degradation and self-condemnation are caused by two
things which are connected with each other: the religious problem and the relationship between the writer and his wife. The
religious conflict is indicated early on in the book when Jörgensen
sees the fireflies in the gardens of Siena as a symbol of the con-
tinuity of nature: "This thought, which was Nietzsche's great
consolation, is a source of horror to me. Always the same pas-
sions, the same suffering, the same tears, the same pangs—always *Ixion* on his wheel, the 'wheel of existence' which the
apostle James also knows. . . . All life and its conditions lie before me—the eternal choice between the earthly music and the
harmony of the spheres—between the fireflies and the stars." [17]

So far Jörgensen has indicated a mental crisis of some kind,
but without going into precise details. More emerges in the
poems with which the work closes. "By the River Eisack," written
in October 1912 after "that strange and sad summer," tells of
the poet's worries, his uncertainty, his fear that after all he was
a child of this world, with thoughts only for his name and
honor, his fear that his will has been divided between "the
earthly roses and the heavenly lily." So far it looks like the old
struggle between earth and heaven which has appeared so many
times in the past, but the last two lines of this poem indicate
that for a time Jörgensen had turned his back on Christianity:
"Lord, I feel how frivolous and hard my heart became when I
turned from the Cross." (Herre, jeg föler, hvor Hjærtet blev let
og blev haardt / siden den Stund, da fra Korset jeg vendte mig
bort.) Already in the previous poem, "Serbian Evening" (Serbisk
Aften), he had used the motif of the Christmas star and told
how he had forgotten his star and only thought of men, but was
now returning to the star again. In both these poems he has
reached an understanding of himself and sees hope before him,
although "By the River Eisack" tells plainly of the difficulties

he encounters. These are still discernible in "November Night"
(Novembernat), in which the old moon symbolism is used
again, despite the final decision to turn away from the world:
"In this moonlit night, this night in November, there dies within
you a soul, a world, a past age." (I denne Maanenat, denne Nat
i November / der döer en Sjæl, en Verden, en Fortid i dit Indre.)
This book, which throughout indicates an intense personal struggle, ends in resolution: the struggle is past. It has been a book
with enormous varieties of mood—ranging from melancholy reflections to the amusing account of the journey to San Galgano;
from enthusiastic admiration for the ancient customs of Siena—
a symbol of life—to the decision to turn his back on the world;
from nature description at the beginning with memories of earlier
techniques to the chastened use of the star motif in the last
poems. Not only does it provide a setting for the life of St.
Catherine, but it fills in the personal background to that book,
a background which seems to dominate parts of it.

IV   Mount Alverno (Alvernerbjærget, 1920)

A third book of a similar nature appeared in 1920—*Mount
Alverno*—a typical Jörgensen travel book full of warmth and
feeling, and not a mere conglomeration of short journalistic impressions such as he sometimes published. It is different from
the other main travel books in that it was not written immediately after the journeys concerned, but several years later. Nor
is it first and foremost an account of two journeys to La Verna,
but a book in memory of Jörgensen's friends there, Father
Samuel, already known from *The Book of the Pilgrim,* to whom
some of the book's most beautiful pages are devoted, and Pico
Pichi, whom Jörgensen met on the first of the two journeys he
here describes. Pichi, who met his death during the First World
War, had translated *The Book of the Pilgrim* into Italian. The
remainder of *Mount Alverno* forms a frame around these two
figures, and corrects and augments some impressions from earlier
works.

Like the other travel books, this is an intensely personal work,
not only by dint of the warmth with which Jörgensen talks of
his old friends, but also because of the autobiographical flashes

in it. In many respects it is "hidden" autobiography, because
the autobiographical elements are couched in an indeterminate
language which leaves the reader with a sense of what has happened, but no precise knowledge of the course of events. For
instance, when talking of the two years which had elapsed between his two journeys to La Verna, he comments:

> Two long years, two strange years, two hard years, when, struck
> blind, I wandered along the edge of an abyss and only awoke and
> came to myself when I slipped over and found myself lying with
> broken limbs at the bottom. I looked up and looked around and saw
> that I was alone—bitterly and finally alone—like a warg in a wilder-
> ness. Alone, but not deserted by everyone. For from among the barren
> cliffs in the valley of bitter tears the good Samaritan came riding
> on his beast and on the she-ass's young colt, and he stopped where
> I lay and did not ask how I had fallen among thieves, but he put me
> on his beast and walked at the side of it himself and led the beast
> by the bridle and did not stop until he reached Salem, the city of
> peace. And in Salem he took me into an inn where he was known
> and sat at table with me and sat opposite me and rejoiced when he
> saw me gain strength and again find a taste for the bread of life
> and the wine of salvation. And from the inn in Salem we went
> together to the Mount of the Transfiguration where it is good to be,
> and where more than anything else we wanted to build three taber-
> nacles—one for the sinner, one for the Samaritan, and one for the
> Master who always lives in the mountain.[18]

With all its biblical references this is a difficult passage to
interpret, as it is doubtless intended to be. More likely than not
it is only intended to be completely understood by the initiated,
not by the general reader. Behind the rather confused symbolism
it is possible to discern Christ the Savior, the friend of sinners,
the giver of life. Yet it is perhaps of some significance that the
period between Jörgensen's two journeys was precisely the time
at which he met Andrée Carof, and it seems more than likely
that the passage also contains a veiled reference to her. Nor is
this the only obscure passage in the book; others are still more
difficult to interpret, and will probably remain so without further
knowledge of Jörgensen's life in Siena immediately after the
break with his wife. On the other hand there is a section on

Dante, telling of his affection for another woman after he had left his own wife and children, which quite obviously has personal implications for Jörgensen.

At other times Jörgensen's digressions—and that is what some would consider such a passage as that on Dante—are the direct result of the powerful feelings which some episode or event produces within him. It would probably not be unjust to Jörgensen's artistry to suggest that when an event really sets his feelings or his memories working, they are sometimes allowed free rein and thus drag the remainder of the work along with them in much the same way as it is said that a novelist's characters often come to live a life of their own, with results which often surprise the author himself. There is an almost explosive force behind Jörgensen's memories and the emotions they produce, and his experience of the feast of the stigmatization of St. Francis in La Verna leads not only to flashes of personal memories, but also to a brief consideration of the moral status of the modern world:

Ah, the midnight office on the night of the stigmatization on the mountain of the stigmatization. Is it possible to give an impression of it to anyone who has not experienced it? Is it possible to write of it so that it will be comprehensible and so that the value of such moments will at least be sensed by those who are at a distance, those who stand outside, those who are indifferent, strangers, enemies? The night of the stigmata—the night of the seventeenth of September— the night when (strange coincidence) Viggo Stuckenberg was born— how have I spent this night all the years of my life before I spent it here? And how is this night, this same night between the 16th and 17th of September 1912 being spent down below in the world which is sleeping or sinning, loving or murdering, while the mountain up here is filled with light and song, keeping watch and praising God? And over the towns below and the mountain on high, the same starry night reigns.[19]

The poet's religious experience leads imperceptibly to his love of reminiscing, which in its turn leads to gentle moralizing, and thus a passage of this nature covers almost the entire spectrum of his production.

V   Journey to Jerusalem (Jorsalafærd, *1923*)

All three elements are also present in the longest of the travel descriptions, *Journey to Jerusalem,* perhaps the most controversial of the books he wrote in this genre. One of the main criticisms was that it was in part more like a guidebook than anything else, with even the prices of meals and transportation included in addition to much practical information for travelers in Palestine. At the end of the second volume he takes his critics to task, arguing that "it does not set out to be a Baedeker," and adding that "many people will perhaps find what they are not looking for and miss what really interests them. But I cannot help that. Someone or other will probably be pleased with something or other in it." In fact, there are two major aspects to the book, the travel account with lengthy descriptions which are interesting in themselves but do not appeal to the feelings, and the expression of what the country had come to symbolize in the mind of a Catholic author.

It is this latter quality which is all-important. Just as *The Book of the Pilgrim* showed how a visit to the native country of St. Francis made the Franciscan movement come to life for him, so *Journey to Jerusalem* makes the Bible live for him in a way it has not done before. Thus the author will often stop in his description of the external features of the country in order to reflect on their religious significance, and sometimes to indicate how he himself relives what has happened in those places. The impression of the Church of the Holy Sepulcher is almost overpowering, while in the chapter entitled "The Shepherds' Field," Jörgensen describes Mass in Bethlehem with a new intensity, reflecting the emotion he felt on hearing it at Christ's birthplace.

Elsewhere—and this is perhaps another ground for criticism—biblical places are used in a completely different way, often to explain something factual which has been puzzling the writer. Thus the strikingly smooth and slippery streets he finds in Jerusalem make clear to him why Christ fell so many times with the Cross, while a visit to Gethsemane on Maundy Thursday explains to him why it was necessary for Judas and his companions to carry torches even though there was a full moon when Christ was betrayed: "The moon rises in the east, over the Dead Sea, and casts its light on the eastern slope of the Mount of Olives, while the western side long remains in darkness. The darkness remains longest, of course, at the foot of the mountain, and that is where Gethsemane is situated. I noted on that Maundy Thursday evening that the moon did not appear over the ridge until about 9.15. But Jesus had probably been taken prisoner long before that time." [20]

Remarks of this nature are openly and avowedly aimed at "certain modern critics," presumably Danes. In general, *Journey to Jerusalem* contains much that is intended to enlighten the writer's fellow countrymen and much, too, which attacks the modern civilization that Denmark of the 1920s was coming to represent for him. Jörgensen is almost everywhere critical of modern cultural trends, but his remarks in this work are particularly biting, and in some ways remind the reader of the polemics from the years immediately after his conversion. It may well be the result of the contrast between the source of Christianity which he was now visiting and the modern country from which he hailed, but his criticism of Denmark is bitter in the extreme throughout the 1920s and 1930s, both in print and in private letters. He has often been represented as a Dane in exile longing for Denmark, but this is only partly true.

He does express his longing in this book, but it is the Denmark of his childhood he longs for. Christmas in Jerusalem gives rise to memories of Christmas in Svendborg, while a boat trip on the Sea of Galilee reminds him of similar trips on the Svendborg Sound. The sight of a Greek school awakens memories of the writer's own school days in his home town, while even the countryside around the Mount of Olives reminds him of the hills around Svendborg: "and when the sun is shining, it all lies in a spring haze, and a white road leads up over the hills and disappears and is the road leading to Galilee, but it could be the road to Græsholmene." He even goes so far when attending Mass on Palm Sunday as to long for the simple service he had known as a child.

In many respects, then, his technique in *Journey to Jerusalem* is the same as before: the book is filled with personal digressions. Likewise, his technique of self-identification also appears here. Elijah in exile, who is no better than his fathers, is an obvious example of this, though Jörgensen does not dwell on this portrait. On the other hand, there is another example of self-identification of a far more complex nature when he tells how, at the command of Sarah, Abraham sends Hagar and Ishmael away. There is an echo of his relations with his wife when he writes: "With a heavy heart, with an unquiet conscience (oh, weak husband, oh, Abraham of a hundred years!) the patriarch gave in to his vengeful wife and arose 'early in the morning' (while Sarah was yet asleep?) and bade Hagar and Ishmael farewell. . . . The mother, the wife, had spoken—the father had no choice but to obey. There he stood, 'early in the morning,' and gave them provisions for their long journey, from which they were never to return. There was nothing else for it—he dared not defy Sarah and her wrath." [21]

However, though the poet here identifies himself with the weak Abraham, he continues by identifying himself with Hagar, the woman who was sent into exile never to return home; he does so in a scene reminiscent of the description of the return of Margerita of Cortona in *On High,* where the weak father is also obliged to give way because of a jealous wife: "Now, on the other hand, there is only one thing to do—to continue, until she reaches Egypt, her native land. Abraham's tent is permanently closed to her and to Ishmael. There is no longer room for them under its low roof of brown, homespun cloth. For in the finest, the innermost room in the tent, Sarah lies with the legal heir in her arms—Hagar can still hear her say, '*My* son, *my* Isaac!' " [22]

The literary quality of Jörgensen's travel books varies enormously. Those which have been considered here contain many traits reminiscent of his best work, and indeed *The Book of the Pilgrim* can be ranked among his best books. All of them, and many of the lesser ones, too, have a typical mixture of lyricism, reflection, factual account, and self-identification. They are peculiarly suited to this mixture, since they allow of much greater freedom than the hagiographies. On the other hand, it can quite well be argued that they allow the writer too much freedom, that he is at his best when the subject in hand puts him under a stricter literary discipline. Certainly *St. Catherine* does this, for in that book the self-expression which must of necessity appear in his writing is buried deep in the foundation, not immediately apparent, and it is doubtful whether he ever attained higher than he did in this work in which such discipline was thrust on him. In the later hagiographies he often resorts to much more open self-expression, as though he has failed to integrate the elements with the same success as previously. Meanwhile, he was first to produce the most personal of all his books, an autobiography in seven volumes.

CHAPTER 5

The Autobiography

THROUGHOUT the period from Jörgensen's conversion to the publication of *St. Catherine*, his works show constant signs of crisis, sometimes financial or domestic, more often of a religious nature. If his work is examined chronologically, it becomes almost painfully apparent that these various religious crises followed one another in rapid succession, though it would scarcely be correct to talk of one constant, protracted crisis. Because of his inventiveness, these crises are expressed in various ways, and thus his literary output cannot be said to be entirely repetitive. However, the influence of Andrée Carof brought Jörgensen within a relatively short space of time to a much more firmly established faith, and in one of his polemical works from the First World War—*The War Pilgrim* (*I det yderste Belgien*, 1916)—he states openly and without reservation that the truth of Catholicism has become "unshakably right and real" for him.

In his autobiography, *The Legend of My Life* (*Mit Livs Legende*, 1916-28, published in an abridged English version under the title of *Jörgensen*, 1928-29), he tells how this came about.

It was no coincidence that this autobiography was written at that particular time, for it was only then that he could look back on his development and see it as a whole. Only now could he feel that the process was complete and the doubts removed. It was written in Assisi, where Andrée Carof had persuaded him to live, during what was probably his most intensely religious period, the time at least during which his religious life found its supreme expression. It was, moreover, written for Andrée Carof, and therefore the account goes no further than the time of their meeting, as he had no reason to take it further. To continue his autobiography for the sake of the general public was

111

a completely different matter, and although later in life he did consider doing so, he realized that the basis for a continuation would be completely different. Meanwhile it is not clear why there should have been a gap of ten years, from 1918 to 1928, between the publication of Book Six and the appearance of the final version of Book Seven. This final volume had originally been written and intended for publication together with the rest of the work, but it was withdrawn; it is useless to speculate on the reason for this, but there is evidence to suggest that Jörgensen was persuaded to change the original draft. Was the long wait for the last volume due to his having lost interest once his original plan was disturbed, or was there a deeper reason? Artistically this last volume does not reach the same heights as the earlier ones, and it was precisely this part of the total work which was most drastically altered in 1949 when Jörgensen produced a slightly abridged second edition of the *Legend* in two volumes. In a letter written to Mogens Kai Nörregaard he complained that this second edition seemed incomplete, and this is particularly true of the final Book, in which there are numerous omissions, while the remainder of the work is substantially the same as before. By way of contrast Jörgensen had written some years earlier that the English edition was the one he liked best; this is an interesting point, since the English edition is considerably more abridged than the second Danish version.

Some writers have compared Jörgensen's *Legend* with the Confessions of St. Augustine or of Rousseau, not so much because of any confessional similarities, but because of the apparently complete openness and frankness of the self-portrait which the work contains, the fearless probing of motives, the total lack of self-idealization. Jörgensen himself compared it with Goethe's *Dichtung und Wahrheit,* which has led other scholars and critics to doubt the authenticity of much that it contains. The very choice of the word "legend" for the title seems also to suggest that not everything should be taken at face value, but that the book is true in its general implication. Until Jörgensen's diaries are made available to the public fifty years after his death (in 2006) it will be impossible to give a complete answer to this problem. Meanwhile, whatever doubts critics might have about the veracity of the *Legend,* it is beyond dispute that the author has not indulged in self-idealization. Indeed, there is sufficient evidence to believe that he has scarcely done himself justice. Likewise, in what must have been one of the most difficult and embarrassing sections, Jörgensen takes upon himself a very large share of the blame for the breakdown of his marriage, hinting that his own inability to manage the family's finances was one of the main causes. There is doubtless some truth in this, but letters written in the 1930s seem to indicate that much of the blame lay with his wife, and that their disagreement was over religion as much as over financial considerations. For an understanding of Jörgensen's work as a whole, such matters have relatively little importance, but they are not without interest when comparing the autobiography with the actual truth. Even if there might be some basis for assertions of self-justification, there is no ground for arguing that Jörgensen has tried to make himself appear better than he was.

The method he adopts in the *Legend* is much the same as in the hagiographies. In both the reader is presented with a portrait drawn from a particular point of view, aimed at stressing certain special characteristics in the person being presented; also the writer allows his imagination to help him when it is necessary to achieve some effect. Thus, the freely invented passages in both *St. Francis* and *St. Catherine* can be compared to the end of the sixth Book of the *Legend,* where Jan Ballin is reading Mass (Ballin was not a priest at the time!), and possibly to the section in the final volume where the poet and the young Danish priest Peter Schindler are out in the Italian countryside. Another technique adopted from the hagiographies is the use of long and very numerous quotations, in the one instance from the writings of the saints, in the other from his own diaries. In each case the object is the same—to quote at length from the "authentic" version, and to give the reader the same opportunity as he had had himself of experiencing at first hand.

One of the points of departure for the *Legend* is Catherine of Siena's idea of *Corde intellegitur:* "we understand what we are worthy of understanding," and also her idea of two forms of love. On the former idea he comments: "No one becomes an atheist unless he has deserved to be one. Everyone believes what he is worthy of believing. I became a freethinker not because

Höffding[1] brought his students up to be freethinkers, but because I was disposed towards it. I became an amoralist and an immoralist, not because Georg Brandes exhorted us to do so, but because my moral qualities were not suited to better things. Only he who has a heart can believe—only he who is good will accept Christianity." [2]

His only excuse for his sinful life, he says, is that no one had taught him what real love was, because everyone was too much concerned with the new philosophy to be bothered with it. It is a surprising assertion, for we certainly have the impression of an affectionate mother from the early part of the work, not to mention Uncle Jörgen, of whom the author speaks with true affection, and about whom he later wrote a short and very beautiful book. Nevertheless, he says that only relatively late in life, through Suso and St. Catherine, did he learn that there are two sorts of love, interior and exterior love. It is through this discovery that he has come to the conclusion that he is devoid of the right sort of love. Although he does not say so at this particular juncture, these thoughts are connected with his relationship with his first wife. Meanwhile he does, in the volume entitled *God's Millstone* (*Guds Kværn*), express himself directly on this subject after discussing the conflicts which had arisen between them: "It is so because it cannot be otherwise. Every man has the life he deserves to have. Every man has the woman he deserves to have. Every man has the love he deserves to have. And he who has taken life in vain and who takes woman in vain and takes love in vain, will find that life will take its revenge on him, and woman take her revenge on him, and love take its revenge on him." [3]

There is a sense of nemesis in this which had probably originated in the ideas of Meïr Aaron Goldschmidt,[4] the Romantic novelist, the second volume of whose autobiography was concerned with a philosophical and historical defense of the nemesis concept. Every action we take in this life will, the argument goes, be punished or rewarded in this life. In the first volume of the *Legend*, when speaking of books he had read, Jörgensen makes admiring reference to Goldschmidt's ideas. At all events, he is here applying the nemesis concept to his own life, and he admits implicitly that he is doing so with reference to his wife. However, if we accept that the *Legend* was written for Andrée Carof, there is also a secondary implication. He doubtless felt a completely different kind of affection for her, the "right" kind of love, and the implication therefore is that he has deserved and been given the "right" kind of woman following the change in the entire basis of his existence.

Put in broad terms, the development he points to is that in his search for truth he has come to realize his own selfishness and has decided to put things right. He has thereby come to appreciate his own lack of love and has sacrificed the happiness which he until 1913 had still believed attainable, for a higher ideal. As soon as he had done that he met, or was led to meet, the person with whom he could share the right kind of love, a love which he talks of in his letters as being completely selfless. It is a series of events of this nature which convinces him of the existence of Divine Providence. This belief in the workings of Providence, working not merely for all creation, but to the ultimate temporal benefit of Jörgensen himself—though not necessarily his physical well-being—is the second main theme of the autobiography, and one, moreover, which he was to develop further in his later hagiography.

If the quotations from his diary which Jörgensen includes in the *Legend* are to be accepted as genuine—and there is no evidence to suggest that they are not—then he must have adhered to the idea of a Divine Providence at a very early age, possibly as a direct result of his reading of Goldschmidt. In an extract dated March 14, 1884, he compares himself with a ship drifting here and there at the mercy of every breath, every change of mood: "And yet I am not afraid, for in the midst of all this I possess the painful yet blissful feeling of the ideal, that God is present on board." [5] In another quotation from the same period he says: "The Father works from without—as Providence." He lists a number of traits from his youth with a hint of Catholicism about them: his predilection for the cathedral scene in *Faust,* the impact which the *Ave Maria* made on him, a list of 25 subjects for study containing eight with a more or less direct affinity with Catholicism; there can be no doubt that all these are included to show that he had been destined from the start to become a Catholic. It is not his intention to show what it was that attracted him to the Catholic Church, but merely to show the presence of Catholic inclinations which he did not recognize at the time. Numerous subsequent events are also explained as being the actions of Providence—the decision to go from Germany to Italy on his first trip abroad, the decision to spend some time as the guest of Mogens Ballin instead of going home to Denmark, the journey to Lourdes in 1909, which introduced him to France, where he was later to meet Andrée Carof. Furthermore, there are other examples implying the intervention of Providence, and in the first edition there are three (in the second edition, two) accounts of dreams or visions of which one, that in which he dreams he is in "the realm of death and the lands bordering on it," has considerable implications for his later development, forcing him to rethink his entire position, his attitudes, and his behavior.[6]

According to these thoughts he was from the very beginning destined to become a Catholic, but that does not prevent him from making a thorough and minute examination of the intellectual reasons for his conversion. He appears to see no contradiction between the hand of Providence and, in this case, the workings of his own intellect. Perhaps his explanation was that Providence led him to experiences which would set his thoughts going in certain directions, thus combining the two aspects. At all events, he treats the entire process of conversion at length, so much so that he was able to write to Mogens Kai Nörregaard that the book was only of interest to non-Catholics. A remark such as this can, of course, imply that he was writing to instruct non-Catholics, or that it was aimed partly at those in Denmark who had been unable to understand his conversion and therefore ascribed it to the wrong motives. Such an objective could well be pursued at the same time as writing for Andrée Carof, and in this limited sense the *Legend* would thus become a self-defense as well as a self-accusation. In this respect it seems that it might owe something to Cardinal Newman's *Apologia pro Vita Sua*, which is also a defense against accusations of having gone over to Rome for the wrong reasons. Jörgensen's *Legend* contains a reference to Newman's book, which in itself shows nothing except that he knew it. However, in their precise formulation of the manner in which they approached Catholicism and gradually realized—almost against their will—that their only way forward was to become Catholics, the two writers are similar, even though their ultimate reasons for looking to the Church were different.

The two main accusations leveled at Jörgensen when he became a Catholic were that he did so for esthetic reasons, because he had fallen in love with the music, the liturgy, the outward show of the Church, and that he was making a good living on Catholic money. He makes no secret of the fact that he was a spendthrift, and that despite a reasonable income his family was often in need. Meanwhile, he stresses that his income came from his journalism, not from Catholic sources. Making a good living was something he scarcely experienced. This is doubtless one reason for his preoccupation with finances in the *Legend,* though it must be admitted that his letters from later in life show that he continued to be concerned with money.

The question of the real reason for his becoming a Catholic is much more complicated, one which even he can only answer within certain limitations. On several occasions it is apparent that he experienced a purely intellectual conviction without being able to *feel* Catholic. His emotions were not involved in the process from the start. He stresses this especially when describing his meeting with the extreme Evangelical Rasmus Clausen, whose ideas were far from Catholic, but whose whole appearance radiated peace of mind, while Jörgensen, whose intellect told him that he was right, knew no such peace. In Book Three, *Italy* (*Vælskland*), he also remarks that the opposition to his Catholic faith came from his feelings, while elsewhere he quotes his diary, where he has remarked: "It is a *torment,* not a consolation, to launch myself out into modern church life—a torment which I suffer for God, so that God can reign and rule in me." These statements are in direct contradiction to others in which he expresses his delight in the Latin language and the beautiful prayer books. He tells how "all the liturgical, ceremonial, decorative side of Catholicism" attracted him and how the plainsong in the churches in Lucca on his first journey to Italy moved him to tears. In one of his letters he also admits that the liturgy played its part in his conversion.

Thus he concedes in the *Legend,* as he had done in the *Book*

of Travel, the attraction he found in the esthetic aspects of
Catholicism, but he strongly rejects the notion that it was this
which made him take the decisive step. After a long review of
his intellectual deliberations, he adds:

I have gone through all this detail, not because the thoughts here
expressed are new (far from it!), but in order to prove that if in those
days I approached Christianity and became a Christian, it was not
because of a fleeting mood, not because of mental intoxication or
anesthetization—it was not for the sake of the incense and the plainsong—but (and alas if it had been otherwise!) it was something
which had been carefully thought out, the result of a piece of serious,
honest, or—if you like—*naive* thought.[7]

It is clear that he moved emotionally in two different directions—attracted by certain sides of Catholicism, repulsed by
others, while the intellectual struggle was going on at the same
time. It becomes equally apparent that Jörgensen only found
peace of mind when he decided that it was impossible to achieve
a complete faith by intellectual processes alone, and that the
only way forward was to make a conscious acceptance of Christianity, an act of the will rather than of the intellect. His intellect had guided him in the right direction, but the final step
demanded resolution rather than thought.

This struggle had been accompanied by another, that between Catholicism and pantheism, which is symbolized by German poetry again, the work of Goethe and Heine in particular,
but also by other German Romantics. This conflict is portrayed
throughout Jörgensen's work, and not merely in the *Legend,* by
the contrasts between the Catholic culture of Italy and that of
Germany which rightly or wrongly stands for pantheism and
Romanticism. In particular, it has already been seen in the *Book
of Travel* how after one disappointment Jörgensen admires the
beauty of the moon, while his companions say their rosaries.
The same type of symbolism is used here in the volume entitled
The Unleavened Bread (Det usyrede Bröd), much of which
takes place in Germany. During a visit to Beuron, the monastery
from which he had fled on his first visit, he stands looking at
the moon and tells the story of a young Dane who wishes to
become a monk. Like Jörgensen, he has come to a monastery,

the symbol of Catholicism, or reality, and stands there admiring the moon, the symbol of pantheism or Romanticism: "'Mr. S., is the moon really your concern?' said an old monk. . . . 'Let the moonlight look after itself, whether it be green or blue. Draw your curtains, say your prayers, and go to bed!' I had felt this conflict sharply the first time I was in Beuron, in the luxuriant bloom of summer. I felt it again now with spring bursting into blossom around me." [8]

Nor is this the only occasion on which he has experiences of this kind: the *Legend* is full of examples of this aspect of Jörgensen's struggle for faith, which are supported by his other works. In both cases the struggle is told more or less indirectly, often with the use of symbols, but it is plain for the eye to see. Even if the autobiography is thought to be "modified" truth, the fact of the protracted and difficult struggle must be accepted, and it must be granted that Jörgensen's reasons for becoming a Catholic were not those imputed to him by his critics.

Despite the use of symbols, it is only to be expected that the writer should be more precise in formulating his experiences here than in his other works, so much so that he says expressly in *Italy* when talking of his great lapse on his first journey to Italy, that he felt "so Germanic and pantheistic." This precision is the more striking if the portrayal here is compared with that in the *Book of Travel*. There are also various inconsistencies between the two accounts which might, if they can be resolved, throw some light on the relationship between the *Legend* and reality. In both works Jörgensen shows how the faith he was beginning to build up was suddenly undermined, but the reasons he gives for this vary. In the *Legend* the poet undergoes a religious experience on the 29th of August and almost reaches the point where he can accept the Catholic faith. But he still has certain doubts, and he is sent to a Professor Pennacchi, who, it is said, will be able to clear up these last points for him. In order to show Catholicism in practice the learned professor takes Jörgensen to a convent and introduces him to some nuns who have been praying for him. Subsequently Professor Pennacchi tells Jörgensen of visits he has had from spirits in Purgatory, and this causes Jörgensen's reaction. In the *Book of Travel* the story is that it is a priest, Pater Felix, who introduces him to the nuns

on the very day of the religious breakthrough. Only after this
visit is he introduced to Professor Pennacchi, who takes him to
Montefalco, shows him the shrine of St. Clara, and tells the story
of the weight of the stones found in her heart. In the *Book of
Travel* this is the cause of the change. Jörgensen was, of course,
perfectly well aware of the difference between his two stories
of the chain of events: the two descriptions of the nuns corre-
spond to each other in broad detail, while in each case Pennacchi
is described as having a face like Baudelaire. Nevertheless, there
is a very great difference between the two accounts.

It is certain that in the intervening period Jörgensen had come
to the conclusion that he had judged Pennacchi too harshly,
and that he had misunderstood the story of the stones. This may
well have caused some change, though scarcely the major reconstruction, and it is worth noting that it is Pennacchi in each
case who causes the reaction. It is perhaps ironical that the
Legend's version gives the account of a vision as the reason for
Jörgensen's revulsion against Catholicism, while the same book
tells of another vision which had far-reaching consequences for
him. It may well be that this irony is consciously produced for
the benefit of Andrée Carof, for whom it should be remembered
that the book was written. Jörgensen is on the one hand making
a conscious effort to tone down his dislike of Pennacchi (in the
following chapter he makes an open apology for what he had
previously written), but at the same time he is ultimately putting
the responsibility for starting the reaction on Pennacchi's shoul-
ders. Exactly what the truth of the matter is, is not clear, and
we might well be forgiven for taking it that it has been modified
in both books to fit in with their different objectives. However, if
the divergencies from the absolute truth in the *Legend* are no
more than this, then it is largely a case of modification to obtain
effects, literary modification, while the essential, inner truth of
the account remains.

As a book of memoirs, the *Legend* can be expected to contain
a large number of reminiscences, which it certainly does. Even
as a boy of sixteen, the poet is seen reminiscing about the previous summer in Svendborg together with the young lady he
always refers to as "her," and who is one of the main inspirations in the novels. Now that that summer is past, he says in

his diary, he can only "make a pilgrimage to the holy places" (Note the terminology even in those days!). In conversation, of course, one memory leads to another, but it is of interest to notice how Jörgensen allows this natural process to develop in the *Legend:* again the technique of letting one thought lead naturally but illogically to another is one he was to experiment with in the later hagiographies, sometimes with surprising effect. In the first volume of the *Legend, The Red Star (Den röde Stjærne),* he writes of memories from his early days in Christianshavn, one of the Copenhagen districts where he had a room, but his eyes are all the time fixed beyond the immediate scene, on Svendborg. Even the windows with their potted plants remind him of home:

Then you walk along the canals, along extensive quays. The water laps between the beams of the bulwarks—with a well-known sound— just as it used to in the evening when you came to the bulwarks in a boat, and the sail was lowered, and suddenly the lapping of the water could be heard under the boat, and its splashing between the piers (then it was scarcely noticed—now it had a new value of its own) seemed to draw, to awaken your longing. And *when* was that in fact? It must have been father who had had us out for a sail— to Taasinge—and we approached Taasinge jetty one clear, dark blue summer evening with white light from the North. . . . Perhaps that was the evening when we were told there were crabs in the boat— but it was not crabs after all—it was father pinching our calves under the thwart—and mother laughed.[9]

This brilliant profusion of memories at two removes is only one of many examples where small, insignificant events remind Jörgensen of Svendborg. Talking of life in Vejle in 1895, he tells that the family went to bed early, without candles—"as we went to bed in Svendborg in former days"—while his birthday in 1906 reminds him of how he had celebrated it in Svendborg in the past. Lake Constance reminds him of the Sound at Svendborg, while the countryside around reminds him of that around Svendborg—in just the same way as these same memories were later to be recalled by Lake Galilee and the surrounding countryside in *Journey to Jerusalem.*

Jörgensen's stay at Überlingen on Lake Constance gives rise

to another of his favorite characteristics, the observation of sound
in the distance at a time of great emotion. It is at a time when
he is going through a crisis, having come to the conclusion that
he is without love, and he sits staring at the lake and noting
all the sound impressions:

> I remain seated. Darkness is falling; it is getting late. Again the
> sound of a steamer—this time it really is the steamer from Constance
> that I came on this morning. . . .
> Then the steamer moves off leaving a trail of foam . . . and silence
> returns. Someone is singing out there on the water—further and fur-
> ther away. Finally that disappears, too, and nothing can be heard but
> the waves washing on the shore and a fish jumping after a fly. Over
> on the dark shore opposite two lamps are still lit. Far down on the
> horizon I can see the glow from the lights in Constance. Now someone
> is rowing towards me on the grey lake—the sound of oars approaches,
> recedes, approaches again and finally dies away. Silence—only the
> distant cry of a bird far out across the water. . . .
> That night in Überlingen—my only night in Überlingen. . . .
> St. Amandus, you the servant of eternal Wisdom, pray for all us
> poor creatures who waver between the false love and the true.[10]

The very close connection between the poet's reflections and
sense impressions is very effective. Not only are there many
sound impressions, but also lights observed in the darkness,
which have previously, especially in the poems, awakened his
longing and his sense of eternity. Time after time his early poems
and novels portray a darkened landscape, symbolical of uncertainty, in the depths of which a light is observed, and now
Jörgensen repeats this technique in his mature work. There are
other examples also, as for instance in God's Millstone when
the author has left his family behind and is sitting in La Rocca,
filled with doubt; suddenly he hears someone singing in the distance, a symbol of the world beckoning to him. The same effect
is produced on various occasions when he is talking of his childhood sweetheart in Svendborg. There is, of course, deliberate
artistry in this, but one quotation from the diary does seem to
indicate that this was an almost instinctive observation for Jörgensen. He quotes his diary to show his feelings during a stay
in Hausen: "Ein stilles, stilles Thal zwischen grünen, sonnigen

Bergen. Kein Laut, nur dann und wann stille, ferne Stimmen und das Schliessen einer Thüre (*sic!*) oben im Felsen."

The *Legend* is a long but very readable book. Not only does it give a penetrating and fearless analysis of the author himself, but it contains many of the most characteristic qualities of his work as a whole. There is poetry in it; there are explanations of various aspects of Catholicism; but there are few signs of polemics. It throws light on the rest of his production, though the rest of his production throws light on it, too. It is indeed the cornerstone of his achievement, and it only really fulfills its function when put in place.

CHAPTER 6

The Later Hagiographies

IN 1909 Jörgensen had been invited to write the biography of Paula Reinhardt. The result was *Die Geschichte eines verborgenen Lebens* (1912), which despite the appearance of a Danish edition under the title *Like a Candle* (*Som en Kærte,* 1931) must be considered among his lesser works. Not only was it a commissioned work, but he was not personally engaged in it, despite his obvious admiration for the otherwise little-known figure he was depicting; any personal elements were spread thinly—and altered in the Danish edition to suit changed conditions. As a whole this book proves that unless he feels a close affinity with his subject, Jörgensen is not at his best, being unable to achieve the true artistry which is present in some of his other books. *Don Bosco* (1929) underlines this. It was also a commissioned work, which Jörgensen was asked to do because of the possibility of Don Bosco's canonization—which in fact took place in 1934.

I Don Bosco (*1929*)

Don Bosco is not a particularly bad work. It contains a number of traits typical of Jörgensen, but there is not the same personal involvement to which we have become accustomed in the books on St. Francis and St. Catherine. It now becomes apparent, if it has not been before, that it is not sufficient for Jörgensen to be treating a person he admires if there is no deeper affinity between them. In many ways Don Bosco was just the person Jörgensen could be expected to be enthusiastic about; he had the firmness of purpose and the willingness to accept self-sacrifice which filled the Danish author with admiration, and his ideals had much in common with Jörgensen's earlier ones. Indeed, Don Bosco's Oratory in Turin must at times have struck him as being a practical example of what he had been advocating in his novel *Our Lady of Denmark* as early as 1900. Jörgensen was aware of the ways in which Don Bosco could be seen as a modern parallel to St. Francis, and this he mentions on more than one occasion. Don Bosco, progressing under great difficulties from a poor home to be the founder of the Oratory, the guardian of hundreds of homeless boys, the founder of a missionary order which has spread throughout the world, was the personification of Jörgensen's ideals of social Catholicism.

And yet there is something missing. Even in his introduction, when discussing his sources, Jörgensen lets it become evident that Don Bosco has not inspired him to the profound study that his two earlier saints had done. He admits that his book is mainly based on two works: *Vie de Don Bosco* by J. M. Villefranche, and *Vita del venerabile Servo di Dio Giovanni Bosco*, I-II, by G. B. Lemoyne. Toward the end he mentions the fact that Lemoyne had also written a nine-volume work on Don Bosco, but it is the shorter one which has been used here. It can hardly be said that Jörgensen has really set about writing a new portrait of the nineteenth-century saint. He must have realized that there is not the same urgency about this book, and in the introduction he talks of the difficulty of writing the life of a man in whom there was no evil, no conflict. This may well have been a difficulty, but in this case there is no doubt that Jörgensen should have added, "and with whom the author can find no affinity."

There is in fact only one aspect of the story of Don Bosco which appeals to Jörgensen's subjective understanding—his faith in Divine Providence. As has already been seen in the *Legend,* a faith in Providence was one of the main tenets of Jörgensen's religious beliefs, a reality which he sees as being of fundamental importance to his own life. This very preoccupation with Providence, stimulating and refreshing as the treatment of it is, has one rather curious effect. It leads Jörgensen to incorporate into *Don Bosco* a lecture he had given in 1902 and subsequently published in his periodical *The Catholic;* it tells of the life of one of Don Bosco's predecessors, Cottolengo, but interesting though his life is, it is scarcely relevant to the subject matter in hand, and thus the chapter emerges as an enormous digression, a sort of hagiography within a hagiography. The main point Jörgensen makes in this chapter is that Cottolengo was completely dependent on Providence, and would consciously work on the assumption that Providence would save him from any difficulties he might incur in his work. Likewise, Don Bosco relied on Providence to an almost incredible extent, quite literally relying on it in his day-to-day life, and time after time finding his faith amply justified. Here, then, Jörgensen and Don Bosco (and Cottolengo) can meet. Thus it is that Chapter XVII, "Providence and Poverty," is that in which Jörgensen reveals his normal literary technique, fusing his own experience with that of Don Bosco. This is by far the most deeply felt chapter in the book. Yet here again Jörgensen was to some extent limited in inspiration, because he had so many facts at his fingertips that he could scarcely indulge his poetic fancy to the extent to which he had been used to doing so. Thus, he recalls various incidents in which Don Bosco's faith in the workings of Providence has asserted itself, but apart from the enthusiasm with which he relates them it would be difficult to discover that they had any personal significance. Early in the chapter, however, he manages a comment which is loaded with personal feeling. Having told how undisturbed Don Bosco was if he discovered in the evening that there was no bread for his boys for the following day, he comments:

So the morning following such an evening he went out to meet Providence. And he met it—simply because he deserved to meet it. There are also others who knock at the door of charity and ask for help for their family sitting at home, hungry, waiting. But how did it happen that the crib was empty, so that the horses now bite and kick each other? Don Bosco had not left his home after a scene with reproaches flying back and forth and doors being slammed—but before he had left his boys he had said, "Go over to the church and pray until I come back." [1]

This reminds us vividly of the indications of family strife in the *Legend*, and seems to show that Don Bosco's reliance on Providence in dire poverty had reminded Jörgensen not so much of his own faith in Providence as of the times when he, too, was suffering want and relying on "something turning up," but without the right attitude of mind. It is an affinity by contrast, rather than the usual feeling of close mental affinity, and this contrast is emphasized later in the same chapter when Jörgensen indulges in the technique he had experimented with on previous occasions, letting the story he is telling merge with his own memories and become something quite different. Don Bosco owes 300 lire in tax and cannot pay; he sits one morning awaiting the arrival of the bailiff, and hears a knock at the door:

> No, it is not he. It is a friend of the house, a lawyer by the name of Occelletti. What has Don Bosco done to deserve this honor? He will soon learn—Occelletti has received a large fee which he had given up all hope of seeing—and he wants to offer Don Bosco a small share of it—"but it is not a lot—only 300 lire!" A boy was sent off at top speed with the money—and caught the bailiff and his men on Österbro Station before they left for Charlottenlund to levy execution. . . . No, what am I talking about—however, the 300 lire arrived just in time.[2]

A reader without any previous knowledge of Jörgensen would be completely mystified by this passage, but the key, if any is now needed, is to be found in the chapter entitled "The Cross" in the *Legend*, telling of Jörgensen's financial difficulties around 1910:

> Just as in the old days at "Saraly" . . . I received at the door of our "Refugium" in Charlottenlund streams of unpaid and unpayable bills, while writs, lawsuits, demands for settlements out of court, executions constantly hung threateningly over my head. I remember one morning in February 1906 when I had just sat down at my desk . . . and the mailman came with a letter announcing that a dissatisfied creditor had arranged for a visit by the bailiff *that very morning*. Without saying a word to my wife . . . [I] hurried to the train and just reached Österbro Station in time to stop the bailiff and his men from leaving for my home.[3]

There is without doubt a certain affectation in this particular passage in *Don Bosco,* though it does illustrate Jörgensen's ability to associate his own experiences with those of the figures he is portraying in his work. On the other hand, he has not succeeded here in entirely merging his own experience with that of Don Bosco, but has deliberately drawn attention to it, much more than was his usual custom.

The effect of this lack of affinity is evident throughout the book. It was one of Jörgensen's convictions that it was necessary to know the surroundings in which the action of his works took place, and consequently *Don Bosco* contains accounts of journeys to Turin itself to visit Don Bosco's Oratory, and to Bechis, where he was born. However, such visits are recounted, much in the style of the travel books, as visits, and the author's impressions of the countryside are not worked into the book to become an integral part of it. The reader is too aware of what is going on: "Now we have told the story of Don Bosco, let us go and visit the place of his birth." This is very different from either *St. Francis* or *St. Catherine,* where the nearest approach we have to this style is at the very beginning when Jörgensen is seen walking through the very streets in Siena where St. Catherine walked as a child.

Throughout the book on Don Bosco Jörgensen uses a more directly personal approach than elsewhere, accompanying his text with direct comments which again almost underline the lack of affinity. He has here to say outright what he wants to say rather than let it emerge from the text. Thus, quite early on, when he is talking about Don Bosco's background and the way in which his father asked for the hand of his mother, he comments, with an echo of an earlier work and an even more distant sound of his own marriage:

Every man wins the woman he deserves; God is indescribably just, scrupulously just, measuring and weighing each grain and quintin as on an apothecary's scale. (Every woman presumably wins the man she deserves, but that is outside my competence.) It is obvious that you will not win a Queen Dagmar with a "May I take you home, miss?" and even if it might be touching that little Gretchen is prepared to leave the door to her room open at night, this willingness to please is not a foundation on which to build a marriage. However good the bread is "when there are none to see," however sweet the "stolen waters"—the old book is right when it urgently warns us against eating or drinking them.[4]

A comment of this sort is at least akin to digression, and

Don Bosco is an outstanding example of the digressiveness for which Jörgensen has often been criticized. Here he certainly does reveal a tendency to wander from the point, to let one thought lead to another and form a lengthy digression before returning to the original point he was trying to make. On the whole, this love of digression is kept within bounds, especially in the more closely knit hagiographies, less so in the travel accounts. In fact, commenting in one place in *Journey to Jerusalem* on this line of criticism, he observes that he is writing the book, and he can do as he likes. In *Don Bosco*, however, digressions are at least as frequent as in the travel books, and more so than in many of them. The mention of a fair gives Jörgensen the opportunity to write a longish description of an Italian fair, pointing out the most striking differences from one in Denmark. This in its turn leads him to wonder what the attraction of such a fair was for Don Bosco as a child, but he hastens to point out that Giovanni Bosco was no Romantic, as the Italians in general are not Romantics, having no word to signify "longing." From this to the German poet Hölderlin, back to Giovanni Bosco, then the repeated assertion that he was no Romantic. He might have been a dreamer, says Jörgensen, but his dreams were not the "blaue Blume" of the German Romantics, but were practical and altruistic. Then he returns to Don Bosco and his decision to perform in the local fair so as to attract attention and thus gather people around him so that he could finish off his performance with a short sermon. This is indeed a long route to the real matter of the passage, occasioned on the one hand by Jörgensen's preoccupation with the differences between northern and southern Europeans, and on the other with his earlier reflections on the conflict between German Romanticism and the reality of Catholicism. Later in the book, pp. 150-51, he also points to the contrast between Heine, for him the personification of German Romanticism, and the Italian Rosmini, while in Chapter III he had previously mocked Heine for seeking in *Nordseebilder* a solution to the riddle of life, again contrasting his hopelessness with the soberness of Don Bosco's conception of the universe. None of these passages is strictly speaking relevant.

Just how much art went into Jörgensen's digressions, it is difficult to say. In the passage mentioning Österbro Station quoted above, a deliberate attempt at artistry is cloaked to look like a natural flow of thought which is suddenly brought to a halt. At the same time, other digressions might well be much more the products of a momentary idea. Certainly some of them have quite an effect on Jörgensen's syntax. Normally he wrote in classically formed sentences, but in his digressive passages the syntax is sometimes broken down, and the sentences might be a series of unrelated observations, or there might be one long sentence covering an enormous span of thought, each section merging with the next without any apparent attempt at order:

And thus it happened that the brave Christians from Murialdo, Bechis, Capriglio (it is well known that the term *cristiano* in Italian is synonymous with the words "human being." A peasant arriving rather late at his neighbor's and finding the wife laying the table, exclaims, "Have *these Christians* not eaten their supper yet?" In J. L. Heiberg's book *Italy* we can read how a shepherd excuses his unruly flock by saying that "of course they are not Christians" i.e. not human beings). However, to return to what I was saying: it happened one evening early in spring, at the end of March or beginning of April, that the churchgoers from Murialdo, Bechis, Capriglio, etc., came walking home from the mission sermon in Buttigliera. The Italian April evenings are as mild as our May evenings: the waysides are turning blue with the small dewy grape hyacinths; the fields are starred with countless thousands of daisies, a little more warm-blooded in their red color than our Nordic camomiles; under the olive trees the corn already stands high and green; the *fava* fields are beginning to flower: soon the bright, black-flecked flowers will send their sweet fragrance out over the path.[5]

Here, at the end of a hectic paragraph with unfinished and broken sentences, the reader is still waiting to know what it is that Jörgensen is starting to relate, and he has to wait through two more paragraphs of reflection and digression before he finds out! The author allows his thoughts to take him away from the beaten track in the first part, but the second part of this digression is occasioned by personal experience, one of the few instances of it in the whole book. Here, for once, Jörgensen can give free rein to his experience and describe not merely the particular countryside around Bechis, which he scarcely knows, but he can talk of Italian nature in general terms, with the warmth and the poetry of personal knowledge. For a brief moment he is in his element, relaxed in a way he seldom is in this book.

Such is the case once more toward the end, during his visit to Bechis. Although this visit is not assimilated into the work as a whole, he feels deeply moved when he stands in the house in which Don Bosco lived his childhood, and in the midst of his reflections there comes the almost inevitable, though not very pronounced perception of sound in the distance: "For a moment I stand alone. From the courtyard below comes the sound of my companions' voices, the chirping of birds from the meadow, a distant call. Then a gentle wind comes and makes the dried maize leaves in the loft at the side of me rustle." [6]

Such moments are few and far between in this book. For all his enthusiasm for Don Bosco, Jörgensen is not at ease in it. His art is there, but it is too obvious and direct.

II Charles de Foucauld (*1934*)

This can not be said of the next hagiography, *Charles de Foucauld,* perhaps the most closely knit of Jörgensen's books, and one in which the personal element is so completely assimilated as to be almost imperceptible. Although the French translation of *Charles de Foucauld* was a success, the original Danish version was an almost complete failure. The reason for this disparity is doubtless the fact that the French were better able to understand and accept a man of De Foucauld's personality, but also that the Danes could not make up for this lack by seeing the personal warmth and emotion with which the book is filled.

Since Jörgensen's meeting with Andrée Carof in 1914, the relationship between them had become one of deep spiritual intensity, a friendship which Jörgensen later claimed was completely devoid of egoism. Through this friendship, Jörgensen came to speak fluent French; it was in this language they always conversed, and in this language, too, that he wrote his diary for a number of years. At the same time, she was responsible for a shift in what might be called his cultural affiliations, moving him from his earlier love of German culture to an increasingly French turn of mind. It was thus a sheer catastrophe for Jörgensen when she died suddenly and at an early age on May 31, 1933. He was now an old man, deprived of his sole companion and of the main source of his spiritual support.

His immediate reaction was to write a short memorial essay which was printed and circulated privately: *In Memoriam Andrée Carof. Sa dernière maladie, sa mort, ses funérailles,* with the significant subtitle, "Il est plus tard que vous ne croyez." This short essay depicts the last days in Andrée Carof's life, from May 25, when it was decided she should undergo an operation, to her death on the 31st. In his grief Jörgensen tells much of the sort of relationship which existed between them, of the optimistic religious views they held, of their love of life and of nature. With increasing pathos he tells of his movements in Foligno during and after the operation, of how he did not realize that she was dying until he was present when she was given Extreme Unction, and of the deep sense of personal loss which her death was to him: "Ce que je croyais impossible est arrivé: Andrée est morte. Mon meilleur ami n'est plus de cette terre. Je suis seul. . . . Que Dieu aie pitié de nous qui l'avons perdue!"

Nowhere has Jörgensen expressed his feelings more potently or directly than in this short work written for a few intimate friends. There is little attempt to sublimate feelings; rather his artistry is concerned with giving as powerful an expression as possible to them, though he still expresses them in a dignified, quiet manner, free from bombast or rhetoric. At the same time he must have felt the need to write of Andrée Carof for a wider public, albeit less directly, and it was with this object in view that he started on *Charles de Foucauld.* Here everything is sublimated, and neither Andrée Carof nor the friendship between her and Jörgensen is mentioned, though there is a dedication to "her who trod Charles de Foucauld's path with me in the Holy Land and in France." Thus far, then, the dedication is plain, though the reader is apt to forget it or to look in vain for any sign of affinity when reading the book.

Born in Strasbourg in 1858, Charles de Foucauld was an orphan by the age of six, and was brought up by his grandfather, a colonel in the French army. At eighteen he joined the military academy of St. Cyr, where his career was anything but brilliant. He was too fond of the good things of life to concentrate on his studies, a *bon vivant* of considerable intelligence but little industry. He became attracted to Africa, and with the approval of his superiors decided to explore Morocco, which at that time was closed to Europeans. For that reason he dressed as a Jew and spent a period of eleven months traveling and exploring and noting his observations. On his return to Paris he underwent a religious crisis, left the army and became a Trappist monk, first in France, subsequently in Asia Minor. Even the rigors of life in a Trappist monastery were not sufficient for him, and after six years he left the Order and settled as an odd-job man at a convent near Nazareth, and later at another in Jerusalem. There he concluded he ought to be a priest, and after taking holy orders he went back, not to Palestine but to North Africa again, where he settled among the Tuaregs. He lived a life of utmost simplicity and poverty, seeking not to convert the Mohammedans, but to civilize the particular tribe he was living with, and achieving considerable esteem among them as a holy man. Finally, he was murdered by fanatics during the First World War.

On the face of it there is little indeed which Jörgensen could find here relating to his own life. De Foucauld was certainly a man who after a dissolute life had undergone a conversion, but relatively little stress is placed on this aspect of his life, and Jörgensen is obviously no longer particularly interested in the phenomenon of conversion which had occupied so much of his attention at one time.

Instead of this type of external similarity Jörgensen finds affinities of a profounder nature, which emerge in two dominant and closely linked themes: Providence and death. The idea of Divine Providence continued to occupy Jörgensen. So far, however, in the *Legend* and in *Don Bosco,* he had been concerned with a Providence which arranged things in such a way that they were immediately seen to be for the best. The *Legend* told how Jörgensen was brought from dissoluteness to a firmly founded religious faith, while *Don Bosco* illustrated the way in which Providence quite literally provided for the justifiable material needs of Cottolengo and Don Bosco. In each case, then, Providence is seen in an optimistic light. Here, however, Jörgensen is forced to look again at his reliance on Providence and

come to terms with a Providence which has inflicted a hard
blow on him:

> In the way it acts, the power we Christians call Providence is some-
> times unpleasantly reminiscent of the ancient Fate or of Atropos
> with her merciless steel. "It often appears," a pious lady in Metz once
> said to me, "that Heaven is not always well informed about earthly
> affairs." Or, as a good Italian woman expressed it: "God is good, *He*
> does no harm. But what is He to do when Fate decrees something?"
> —Fate—*il Destino*—is the highest authority, against which even God
> struggles in vain. . . .
>   And yet there is a Providence behind Fate—even when an earth-
> quake shakes half India and crushes thousands of people in the cities
> it destroys. There *is* a Providence—the Lord's Prayer says so, the
> Church teaches it, we Christians believe it. In the Roman Missal there
> is a collect for the seventh Sunday after Pentecost which begins: "O
> God, by whose unerring providence the world is ordered"—Deus,
> cujus Providentia in sua dispositione non fallitur— . . . Until a year
> ago I had seen this prayer in my book, presumably read it, but with-
> out paying special attention to it. Since I have prayed it, and now I
> know what Hans Christian Andersen knew when he wrote *The Story
> of a Mother*.[7]

Accepting Providence is in fact here almost synonymous with
resignation, which in itself is the key word in Andersen's tale,
and these two ideas are constantly intermingled throughout the
book. "Let us be sad, but let us thank God for this sadness,"
says De Foucauld on leaving his sister's home immediately before
entering a monastery. Later in the book this resignation is given
a more positive turn with the significance not merely of accepting, but also of doing the will of God: "I want nothing but what
You will. Once and for all, Lord, I have surrendered my will to
You, and I will never take it back—it has for ever been submerged in Your holy will. . . . Let everything happen as You
wish; let everything happen, whatever it is You wish to
happen."[8]
    Finally this positive desire to do the will of God leads to the
attitude in which De Foucauld is able to thank God for the past,
even if he is at the moment undergoing the pain of taking leave.
It is when he has decided to leave Nazareth, the goal of his
longings, that he sees that he has enjoyed great grace in being

able to live there, and that he will never be able to thank Providence enough for having led him there in the first place. There is a good deal which points to Nazareth having a significance for De Foucauld similar to that of Assisi for Jörgensen, and this particular passage tends to emphasize this.

Having taught himself resignation, De Foucauld goes on in some measure to teach it to the Tuaregs, more particularly to the slaves whom he meets but is unable to help: " 'Life is short,' he says to his brothers in chains, 'Allah has *written* that life shall be full of suffering for you, but if you behave well he will give you Heaven. It is not your lords, nor the merchants who stole you who have put you into slavery—God has ordained it so; He has *written* that you shall be slaves, and He has done it for your own good, for He is good and only wishes well for mankind.'—There is nothing else for it—for slaves (as for all of us) —but to submit to the holy, incomprehensible will of God." [9]

In talking of resigning oneself to the will of God, or to Providence, Jörgensen keeps to fairly general terms, envisaging all the many facets of life which can make it unbearable. The particular aspect he himself was battling with was, of course, death, and thus it is not surprising that there is a constant recurrence of the theme of death throughout *Charles de Foucauld*. It emerges first in the account of De Foucauld's life as a Trappist, in the greeting of the Trappists, "Remember, Brother, that you must die," and subsequently in the quotations from his letters, when he talks of death's being attractive, and of wishing to leave "this earthly exile." To this Jörgensen comments that death seemed to the 33-year-old De Foucauld to be the only goal worth striving for: "while, as for the rest of us . . ." The same thought recurs later on the same page when De Foucauld is leaving France, and his thoughts go back to the monastery he has left and to his sister's home "among the green hills of Burgundy, to the mansion in the great park, to the quietly babbling Ouche and to the tall poplars by the green canal where the boats slowly glide from lock to lock." [10]

In De Foucauld's diary from Nazareth, especially from the period before the Easter he spent there, the idea of death is again present throughout, and in his reflections on how quickly Christ's thirty-three years had passed, the reader senses that

Jörgensen is reflecting on how soon and suddenly Andrée Carof's
death had come. This is closely followed by a short account of
how De Foucauld was once waiting for a visit from a close
friend, but instead received the news of his death. Finally, of
course, his own death comes suddenly and unexpectedly: "Then
the end came, and came suddenly, as it usually does with those
whom God loves." The significance of this sentence is in the
second half, and even more significantly the account of De
Foucauld's murder is preceded by the motto with which Jörgensen had prefaced *In Memoriam Andrée Carof*, "Il est plus
tard que vous ne croyez." The book is both a memorial to Andrée
Carof and a *memento mori* in itself. Jörgensen was now experiencing in reality that idea of *tutto passa* which had been one of
the principal motifs in *St. Catherine*.

Outstanding among the passages concerned with death is that
touching on the Good Friday liturgy, mentioned in connection
with De Foucauld's Easter in the Holy Land. It is striking not
merely because of the intensity of this particular passage, but
also because of the literary treatment it is given, which is a
further key to the understanding of the work. He writes first
about the moving liturgy of Holy Week, telling how the shadow
of the Cross moves closer each day, until on Good Friday it
stands "alone and high," as St. Bridget saw it in one of her
visions. Then, however, the scene shifts from Palestine to Assisi,
and the next page and a half is concerned with the scene in
the cathedral on Good Friday, a scene which is obviously based
on personal reminiscences of how the author himself had experienced the Good Friday ceremonies. He does not mention Andrée
Carof, but it is an established fact that this intense experience
was one which he had shared with her, and the climax of the
scene with the final prayer, "Lord have mercy on us poor sinners," seems to be a half echo of the end of *In Memoriam*: "Que
Dieu aie pitié de nous qui l'avons perdue!" After this exclamation the scene immediately moves back to Ephraim in Palestine.

This technique of shifting from one scene to another has been
met before, and it becomes a feature of Jörgensen's later work.
In this particular book it has a special significance, as it is often
directly concerned with the ultimate source of inspiration—
Andrée Carof. Precisely the same method is adopted when De

Foucauld is living as a hermit at Beni-Abbes and has received a visit from Monsignor Guérin of the White Fathers, under whose jurisdiction he is working. De Foucauld has enjoyed having company, but now he is alone again:

> Charles de Foucauld was never a sentimental man. And yet there is a turn of phrase which just in these early lonely years keeps returning in his letters: "Je suis seul,"—"I am alone." Despite his love of the desert he, too, had felt the truth in the expression *Vae soli,* "woe to him who is alone."
> Charles de Foucauld goes inside—he is alone. On the table there are still the remains of his last meal with his friend: barley bread, dates, a half-empty tin of condensed milk. Charles de Foucauld looks at the chair in which his guest was sitting only half an hour ago— now it is empty and will remain empty for who knows how long. Tomorrow the lonely meals, the most difficult times of the day, will start again—lonely, because even if he lets little Abd-Jesu eat together with him, it is not the same as having someone to speak intimately with, someone of whom one can ask advice, or even someone to whom one can tell all the small happenings of the day—"Gubbiotti was standing in the doorway as usual, more ragged and out-of-work than ever—Chiara Falcinelli came and told me she is to go into hospital for an operation—Angelina has no more firewood; she says one bundle will be enough." [11]

Not only are the reflections on loneliness and an empty chair obviously the fruits of personal loss, but the change of scene to the everyday life in Assisi shows clearly where Jörgensen's thoughts really were when he wrote this passage. His own personal life intrudes on the scene he is portraying, asserts itself for a time, and then is again submerged in the main narrative.

The same sort of thing happens when Jörgensen is writing about the home of De Foucauld's sister at Barbirey. Barbirey lies very close to Velars, where Andrée Carof owned a house. Not only did Jörgensen know the district, but he had also visited the De Blic family together with Andrée Carof; thus, when he tells of De Foucauld's arrival there, he is in fact telling of his own memories from a district which meant a lot to him:

> A narrow gauge railway leads up through the valley to Epinac les Mines, and a couple of times a day a modest train stops gently and

carefully at the tiny stations with the lovely names—Plombières, Velars, Fleurey, Sainte-Marie, Saint-Victor. But before it reaches Saint-Victor there is Gissey, and if Monsieur de Blic knows you are coming, he will be at the station. But it is almost more amusing to surprise him, and in Gissey, near the old bridge over the Ouche, there is a little inn where you can get a golden omelette, white bread, good red wine (you *are* in Burgundy, you know!). Then you go over the bridge, and there is a beautiful road along the Ouche—the delicate foliage of the willows hangs down in the clear water; the bank is lined with flowering rushes; a kingfisher darts across the water in a blue flash. . . . And then you are in Barbirey and walk across the great courtyard of the mansion and ring on the main door, and Mademoiselle de Blic, always dressed in black, herself comes and opens the door and takes you into the huge hall with the hunting trophies on the walls, and she chides you for not having written. And Monsieur de Blic is in his library and shows you his latest acquisitions —it is especially original editions from the eighteenth century he collects.[12]

Nowhere does Jörgensen say that he himself has been to Barbirey, but a passage such as this shows clearly that he has a personal knowledge of the scene. Without it he could not have written in such detail, or with such gentle poetry. And each time he returns to Barbirey, it is to the accompaniment of a rather more lyrical, intimate style than he uses elsewhere, one showing personal knowledge and also perhaps underlining the fact that it had a personal, private significance for him.

Thus the real character of this memorial to Andrée Carof begins to emerge. Jörgensen chose not to write a book about her herself, but true to the principle he had adopted in his best works of hagiography, he had looked for a figure with whom he had an affinity. Only this time he looked for someone with a close affinity with Andrée Carof, and found him in Charles de Foucauld, a man with close connections with the very parts of France with which she herself had been associated—the upper bourgeoisie of Paris and more especially Burgundy. In addition to that, Charles de Foucauld had ideas which were not unlike those of St. Francis of Assisi, as is pointed out on various occasions, and here it is well to know that Andrée Carof herself had undergone a religious awakening in which St. Francis had played a considerable part. Finally, De Foucauld had spent much of his life in Palestine, which Jörgensen had also visited with Andrée Carof, and this gives him the opportunity to refer to one of his own books, *Journey to Jerusalem,* in which she figures. All these quite noticeable points of contact between Jörgensen and the figure he is portraying are accompanied by the echoes of the personal struggle he was undergoing while writing this book, his struggle to accept a difficult decision of Providence, and an attempt to come to terms with another's death and with his own loneliness. *Charles de Foucauld* emerges thus as a book charged with emotion, but it is most carefully controlled. So successful was Jörgensen in concealing his torment in a time of profound trial that his book was in danger of being completely misunderstood when it was published in Denmark, where, indeed, it is still among the neglected masterpieces.

III   St. Bridget of Sweden (Den hellige
Birgitta af Vadstena, *1941-43*)

The affinity between the author and his character in *St. Bridget of Sweden* is of a very much more obvious kind, and Jörgensen himself said that he could understand her well because they both came from the North, lived in Italy for a large part of their lives, and gradually became "italianized." However, it is scarcely an affinity of temperament, but rather one of surroundings. Bridget is a woman born in Sweden who grows up in a purely Swedish milieu, imposes a voluntary exile on herself, and following a youth actively engaged in the Swedish life of the day she spends the rest of her life in Italy. There she gradually takes a greater and greater part in the cultural life of the South, becoming not only a widely recognized influence there, but also a center of attraction to people around her, pilgrims and natives alike. Most of those who flocked around her probably only came to see the "giraffe," Jörgensen remarks when crowds throng around Bridget in Cyprus, significantly enough using an expression he applies to himself in one of his letters. From his own experience he was only too well aware of what it meant to be a famous person; he, too, had received streams of pilgrims and tourists in his house in Assisi, and he could sense what Bridget had gone through in this respect. "Good day, I am a Scandinavian!" is a greeting from one of her many callers, and this is certainly an echo from Jörgensen's own days in Assisi, while elsewhere he bases himself on his own experiences and reflects on how much mail Bridget would have received had she achieved comparable fame in the twentieth century. Although he would not and indeed could not say so in so many words, the affinity between Bridget and Jörgensen is not merely that they both had gone from the North to live in Italy: it is also the fact that they both had achieved international fame down there. Here is the deeper layer of affinity between them.

On a different level Bridget and Jörgensen have similar experiences in their travels through Italy and elsewhere as pilgrims, visiting the holy places, and coupling their visits with thoughts on their significance. A further likeness is the fact that they both visited Jerusalem and the Holy Land, and Jörgensen is again able to sense, through his own experience, what this journey must have meant to Bridget, and is thus able to supplement her own account of it.

There does not, on the other hand, appear to be any question of showing that Bridget gradually acquired Italian characteristics during her many years in the South. She learned to speak the language and to understand the Italian society she was living in, but she did not become italianized in the sense of becoming an Italian by adoption any more than Jörgensen did himself. For all his love of Italy, he remained very Danish in many respects, and his Danishness is symbolized by his return to his native town shortly before his death. Similarly, Bridget always felt herself to be a Swede, and on several occasions we read that her thoughts turned to Sweden, to Vadstena in particular, and of course, the book finishes with the return of her remains to Vadstena for burial. Self-imposed though her exile was, she constantly felt the bonds which existed between herself and Sweden, and she was aware of the problems of her friends and relatives there, for whom she could do little from such a distance. Here, too, the general situation is reminiscent of that of Jörgensen, though it is not possible to point out any direct parallels.

Significantly, it is while portraying Bridget in Italy that Jörgensen makes most of his more or less openly personal allusions.

It is in Italy that he feels an affinity; there is not much evidence of it in the portrayal of Bridget's early years in Sweden, though the fact that she is shown to be a Franciscan tertiary in the first volume might well be an indication of the author's search for self-identification. Similarly, the gradual transition to the first person while describing Bridget's pilgrimage to Nidaros seems to be something of the same order. On the other hand, nowhere does he dwell sufficiently long on any aspect for it to be obvious self-identification, not even when he seizes the opportunity of mentioning Velars in talking of the possibility that Bridget might have gone through the area around Dijon on her first pilgrimage to Compostella.

St. Bridget's life is easily divisible into two main periods, that in Sweden and that in Italy, and thus it is natural that the first volume of this study should close with her departure from her native land for Italy. A departure is a common occurrence in Jörgensen's work; he had known many of them and was inclined to dwell on them. Thus, too, it is natural enough to open the second volume with some remarks on Bridget's feeling of separation from those she has left behind. We are straightaway led into the new Italian world, and all her experiences there are seen in the light of Jörgensen's own, even to the apparently chance comment that "in Siena the women are fairest," which reminds the observant reader that that had been Jörgensen's own opinion some thirty years before. Bridget comes to Rome and receives news from home; she undergoes doubts as to her true calling in life; she sees spring there and experiences it through Jörgensen's eyes. She visits Portiuncula and there feels the same doubts as those Jörgensen describes in the *Book of Travel*, while her financial difficulties also seem to strike a familiar chord. These, and other episodes like them, are spread throughout the entire second volume, and in their very sporadic nature they mirror the particular type of affinity which is playing its part in this book.

Elsewhere the presence of the author becomes more immediately obvious, though still in sporadic fashion. Twice in the second volume Jörgensen turns to the way in which the Italians spend their evenings. The first occasion is when Bridget is spending the evening together with her daughter Karin and her son

Birger in Campo de' Fiori. It is the sort of scene Jörgensen himself knew well; he points out that most Italian families meet in the kitchen, pile olive branches on the fire, and talk about the events of the day. Perhaps, he says, some old woman or other will mumble a song about St. Anthony—and goes on to recapitulate the contents of one such song: "Grandma Ursula sings, and we listen with a more or less sceptical smile. And then the fire burns low, and the last embers are gathered together for the bed warmer." [13] The technique is similar to that seen before, the gradual change from third person to first where the scene in fact is one the author is basing on his own life. The process is repeated some fifty pages later in the account of Bridget's last evening together with Bishop Thomas of Vexjö:

> Those who know Italy and have lived together with Italians will know that the fireplace is the focal point of an Italian house—as it used to be with the ancient Romans. After a cold winter's day or a cool spring day someone will usually say on leaving the dinner table: *Andiamo al fuoco,* and for many families this means: "Let's go into the kitchen!" For there and there only there is a fire for them to warm themselves by! In many places the fireplace is so wide and so deep that there is room for a narrow bench on either side of it. There sit old Grandma Maria and Grandma Ursula warming their wrinkled old hands over the glowing coals. But it is not always wise to sit too close to the fire—now and then Rigo comes with his arms full of olive branches or dry vines which he has cut off—now is the time to *potare,* to prune both the olive and the vine—and then the dry tinder crackles and flames up, and the sparks shoot out and settle on the women's skirts and must quickly be brushed off before they burn a hole.[14]

It is clear that the two scenes are not quite identical, though they are very similar. What is interesting is the fact that a Grandma Ursula is mentioned in each of them. All the Italians mentioned are in fact real, the family with whom Jörgensen stayed. Rigo was his landlord, and the old women were Rigo's mother and mother-in-law. Again, then, this is an example of Jörgensen's capacity for letting one scene merge into another because of the affinity between them.

There is, however, little common ground between Bridget and Jörgensen as far as personalities are concerned. She is shown to have been another of those powerful, even domineering, female characters to whom Jörgensen looked up. She has the same strength of character as Catherine of Siena, but it is probably true to say that she lacks the warmth with which the Italian saint was also endowed, and which made her attractive to Jörgensen. She does not make quite the same demands as Catherine; she expects less of people, but demands that they are entirely consistent in their Christianity, and when she sees reason to condemn them, she is generous in the punishments she metes out to them in her apocalyptic visions. Something of her effect on Jörgensen can be seen from his letters to Mogens Kai Nörregaard. On May 1, 1939 he remarked: "I am having difficulties with Santa Brita—she is so absolute in her demands, and her Hell is so subtle in its cruelty. (So is Dante's—but 'la Divina Commedia' only pretends to be fiction, not revelation)." Nörregaard has pointed out in conversation that Jörgensen was actually afraid of Bridget, and this conception is supported by a letter written on July 9, 1939: "I am working on Santa Brita as much as I can. But something seems to have gone completely wrong for me—I have actually begun to feel sympathetic towards poor Magnus Smek whom, on behalf of God, she calls 'a crowned donkey' with 'the heart of a hare.' She cannot have been easy to get on with. And she was always right—which is a feminine characteristic." It is striking that Jörgensen, who in the past had suffered from weakness of character, should be able to understand and sympathize with this weak-willed king of Sweden who gave in to any and every influence which was exerted on him. There is no trace of identification between the two; Jörgensen had changed too much for this, but he could see—while Bridget could not—the human side of the king's weakness.

On the other hand, he makes no attempt in the book to show his disagreement with Bridget or indeed to analyze her character as such. On the whole, he is content to tell of what she did, but he evinces little interest in discovering why she did it. The reader of this book must wonder at times what personality lies behind the sadistic visions of hell and purgatory, behind the many allegories using animal forms, behind the round condemnations for what today would scarcely be considered faults. Although Jörgensen on occasion shows himself to be aware that

Bridget is sometimes using the vision as a literary medium, he
does not venture to consider where, if anywhere, the line can
be drawn between the two phenomena. He talks, for instance,
of the types of allegory Bridget uses, and says such things as
that "Bridget goes so far in her allegorizing," thus indicating
that he realizes she is making a conscious composition. Yet when
he reproduces her vision of the birth of Christ and the childhood of Christ, all of which resembles a meditation rather than
a vision, he is content to point out that it reminds one in some
ways of the apocryphal gospels, but he does not go on to draw
any conclusions from this. In other words, he limits himself to
generalizations, and even when returning to the theme of inspiration on which he had touched in *St. Catherine*, he limits
himself to admitting that outside elements can be mingled with
what is inspired from above, and elsewhere he gives what in
fact is an example of this when pointing out that Bridget's conception of society can have had some influence on her condem-
nation of King Magnus Ladulås.

Nor does Jörgensen really tackle the problem of how reliable
Bridget's *Revelations* are, although the second volume of his
work does contain a short passage in defense of them. Bridget
dictated in Swedish, but Alphonse of Jaen, who knew no Swedish, did the final edition and Latin version. As Jörgensen points
out, Bridget's Swedish confessor, Petrus Olai, was not pleased
with this arrangement, but he makes no effort at all to discuss
the two interrelated problems of whether there might have been
misunderstandings, or whether Alphonse might conceivably have
included anything in the *Revelations* which had not originally
come from Bridget.

A hagiography is perhaps not a piece of literary or psychiatric
analysis, but both the question of Bridget's personality and the
reliability of her visions and revelations would seem to require
a critique or treatment in some form or other. The fact that they
do not receive it has led to the accusation that Jörgensen is
uncritical in this final hagiography. In a way, of course, this is
true, as indeed it is in the others, though less obviously so. On
the other hand, it can be said in his defense that he shows
himself aware of the problems of authenticity and veracity even
if he does not discuss them at length, and it must be assumed

that he did not discuss them because he did not feel justified in doing so. This is a problem which he feels is beyond him, and he prefers to leave it unanswered. This is very different from an uncritical acceptance of everything.

Nor is it really Jörgensen's purpose to discuss and analyze in this way. Rather, he sets out to portray the Middle Ages and a medieval personality on the basis of the Middle Ages themselves. He wants to show their world, their ideas, their way of life from their point of view, not to criticize and evaluate them from a twentieth-century standpoint. In fact, with his constant awareness of the plight of the twentieth century he is sometimes apt to judge the present day through the eyes of the Middle Ages. In this aim of depicting the Middle Ages through its own eyes, he is supremely successful. Because of what he points to as the unity of Europe in the Middle Ages, and because he has to show and explain Bridget's activities in a geographical area ranging from central Sweden to southern Italy, he is faced with the task of controlling an enormous mass of complex material— the political situation in Sweden, the war between England and France, Italian politics, the position of the Pope in Avignon, the actions of the Holy Roman Emperor. Names of kings, prelates, heretics, all of whom would be more or less unfamiliar to his modern readers, have to be included in such a way as to be of significance. The favorite places of pilgrimage in the Middle Ages had to be brought to life for an age in which Catholics made pilgrimages elsewhere and largely in a different spirit, while non-Catholics were not interested in pilgrimages in any case. Here again Jörgensen includes a vast number of legends connected with those holy places, also without making any attempt to decide how much is acceptable and how much merely belongs to the realm of the medieval imagination. If all this were to be subjected to a literary, historical, or archeological examination, the book would become completely unreadable. It should be remembered that it is a work of literature, using literary methods, and as such it is an outstanding portrayal of the Middle Ages. Where necessary Jörgensen has supplemented his medieval sources with fictional events or personal reminiscences. The arrival of Pope Urban V at Genoa on his return to Italy, although based on a historical source, is a reconstruction, as is the funeral of Bridget's father Birger in Uppsala, but Bridget's experience of Rome in Holy Year is based on what Jörgensen himself had seen in a Holy Year in the twentieth century.

One aspect in which Jörgensen and Bridget resembled each other was in the fact that both were moralists. Despite the unfortunate overtones of that word today, it is true to say that Jörgensen is a moralist throughout his Catholic writings, making the most of every opportunity to draw a moral for the twentieth century from his medieval portraits, though rarely spending so much time on it as to make his remarks indigestible. Thus Bridget's attempts to mediate between England and France during the Hundred Years' War have a special significance for Jörgensen during the Second World War. Her vision of England and France as two animals seeking to devour each other, but only succeeding in destroying each other, becomes an allegory of England and Germany trying to do the same. Swedes seeking refuge on the island of Gotland during political disturbances in Sweden echo the plight of Danish refugees in Sweden. But war is not the only modern problem Jörgensen looks at; true to his custom he touches on a whole range of modern social problems and comments on them in turn: birth control, the increasing pace of modern life, the position of an age without a faith. And all this is accompanied by an apologetic element in which the author directly defends certain aspects of Catholicism and explains others which were likely to be foreign to a non-Catholic public. Thus, the practical purposes of his book are perhaps more obvious than has been the case in any of the earlier hagiographies. Paradoxically, the author's increasingly intense preoccupation with the Middle Ages has sharpened his awareness of the weaknesses of the age in which he lives, and this awareness forces itself into his writing.

This by no means implies that *St. Bridget* is a prosaic book in which poetry and beauty have no place, though it is less poetic than, for instance, *St. Catherine*. Even the mention of the area around Dijon, which in *Charles de Foucauld* leads to a lyrical interlude, has no such effect here. This lack of adornment is in line with a general movement toward greater abstraction and simplicity which had taken place in Jörgensen's prose and poetry over the last few years. As in his poetry, so in his prose he was seeking to produce his effect by more and more artless means, and his momentary glimpses of nature are but short: "Then we follow the little stream running past the farm to the lake—the Björken. The meadows stretch clover-green to the reeds on the edge of the lake. There is a scent of clover and goose-grass; a cow bell rings a little distance away. Blue the heavens stand above the silent, green countryside." [15]

Jörgensen has abstracted the essentials of this miniature, the colors, the scents, the sounds, and by the inversion in the final sentence—which is more successful in Danish than in English—he emphasizes the overriding blueness of the sky. It is, as in the shorter poems, a piling up of choice detail to give an overall impression, and gives a brief glimpse of the writer's consummate artistry. Thus it comes as something of a surprise when the description of the landscape around Ulfåsa turns out to be more akin to Jörgensen's earlier nature description, deliberately seeking to evoke a mood:

> The years passed. Spring came to Ulfåsa, and the birches stood in their delicate, pale green foliage against the black firs; autumn came to Ulfåsa, and the foliage on the birches hung like a golden ornament over the dark background of the deciduous forest. The winter innocently brought its snow year after year, and the summer came with its light nights and was not ashamed to look the same as last year. The blackbird sang at dusk in the long summer evenings, and every Christmas the yellow-hammer, the great titmouse, and the shrike gathered around the sheaf of corn in the courtyard of Ulfåsa.[16]

A further examination of Jörgensen's work, however, shows this to be taken in its entirety from his earlier essay on St. Bridget in *Pictures of Roman Saints*. In its creation of mood it is in striking contrast to the remainder of *St. Bridget*. Nowhere in this book does the countryside create the desire to travel afar, as it does in *St. Catherine*. Nevertheless, the description of the countryside around Assisi is more subjectively colored than most, as was to be expected, though the evocation of mood is the result not so much of the tangible description as of the eulogy of the Italian summer as a whole:

High summer, *solleone*, when the sun stands in the sign of the lion —fiery July of which Carducci has sung: "What summer there is in July. Song rises like love over the plain where the harvest is being gathered."—It is the lilting song of the harvesters which is always a song about love, a *stornello d'amore*. Work and love, *lavoro* and *amore*, the Italian summer burns in both these words. July is a month of white heat, a month of fire—those who sit inside behind closed shutters and see the sunlight like a white glare behind the green slats of the venetian blind might almost be afraid of it.[17]

These are the author's memories of Italy, written down in Denmark. They are the memories of an old man who was not sure whether he would ever go to Italy again. Perhaps it is inevitable that there should be a little wistfulness present in this long work, which he knew would be his last large-scale book, so large that he was never certain he would be able to finish it. He was aware of this, and referred to this final section as being the most difficult for him. Much more the mark of an old man is the fact that he so often refers to the judgment pronounced on a man's life. "Every man finally ends in his life in the place he has fundamentally wanted to reach," [18] he remarks once, while he also talks of everyone pronouncing his own judgment on himself; Heaven and Hell, he maintains, are every man's own doing, and Bridget asks people to review their lives in the light of the possibility of their soul's being required of them that night. This, he maintains, is her constant theme, but we can wonder whether it is not also a theme with special significance for the biographer. It keeps recurring with considerable persistence, though it never reaches the status of a leitmotiv, as does St. Catherine's demand that every man shall enter the cell of self-knowledge, and her insistence that every man is faced with a choice.

St. Bridget of Sweden is a very considerable achievement, a *tour de force* in Jörgensen's production. It stands out because of its breadth, its epic quality, though it lacks the warmth of *St. Francis* and the intensity of *St. Catherine*. The limited sense of affinity which Jörgensen felt with St. Bridget was not sufficient to ensure either of these. Instead it has a grandeur and splendor of its own; it is the work of many years of research and reflection, and constitutes a fitting conclusion to Jörgensen's prose writings.

CHAPTER 7

The Poetry

ALTHOUGH Jörgensen considered his prose works to be the most important part of his writings, it is on his poetry that his reputation in Denmark mainly rests. Appearing at fairly regular intervals of time, and consisting of poems written on the whole not as units of a larger collection, but as individual comments and reflections, these volumes provide an interesting and valuable commentary on the mental and religious development portrayed in the prose, as well as being of impressive beauty and artistry in their own right. Jörgensen's poetry and prose are complementary to a very high degree.

I Verse (Vers, 1887)

The poems in the first volume, *Verse,* are highly autobiographical, and give a clear insight into the poet's state of mind when he started writing his cycle of short novels. They show his reactions to his upbringing, to his childhood aspirations, while at the same time he is shown still to be bound by that upbringing. "Alas, those childish dreams, I thought they were dead," he comments, as he realizes that he cannot make a break with his past. Even the new life, the radical, Promethean path he had chosen, is only a dream, and with this realization comes a feeling of dissatisfaction, of frustration, which on the one hand leads him to turn his back on everyday life and seek consolation in nature, and on the other to hate all signs of hope and life which he sees in others. In a poem entitled "Easter" ("Paaske"), in a setting reminiscent of one scene in his novels, he tells how he was going home by train one Easter morning, tired and lonely, watching the trees springing into life outside, and the happy holiday crowds out to enjoy themselves: "I hated these festive and happy crowds / passing by with their plebeian

149

smiles, / I hated the base language of their gestures / and the coarse public-house style of their joy in life."

The most powerful expression he gives to this feeling of hatred of a superficial life of forced gaiety, occasioned by his own insufficiency, of course, is in the impressively rhetorical "Faust's Words to Spring'" ("Faust til Foraaret"), where the disconsolate Faust expresses his loathing for all the promises of the spring and curses them with all the intensity he can muster.

Instead Jörgensen turns to nature, and in the pantheistic "Prayer" ("Bön") tells in highly figurative language how he is seeking an escape from himself: "I come to you, oh, eternal mother, tired in soul and in mind, / The tempest has driven the ships of my dreams against the rocky coast, / and the surf which played with the wreck still rolls— / The festive delight is dead in my breast, the temple I built to myself, / and humbly I come now to the vault of your church / to pray where the tempest is the organ, and the heaven the roof."

The tone is easily recognizable from the earlier novels, and the poems in this volume, which Jörgensen in the *Legend* called "eighty pages of melancholy in verse," center on the themes of loneliness, disgust, death, and powerlessness.

Stylistically the poems of *Verse* are very ornate, and the word "baroque" has been used of them. Jörgensen experiments with compound words and phrases reinforced by strong alliteration:

Hver sölvskællet Stjærne, der svömmer i Nathimlens sorteblaa Hav,
hvert sitrende Savn, der drömmer ved visnede Vaardages Grav.

(Every silver-shelled star swimming in the black-blue ocean of the night sky, / every trembling want, dreaming at the grave of withered spring days.)

Nature is personified, and windows are given new personal attributes: they are "blind" or "anxiously staring." At the same time Jörgensen the naturalist tries to achieve something like scientific accuracy in his work, sometimes with a less than fortunate effect, as in the famous metaphor "the thought-fostering leaves of the flower of my brain," but sometimes in much more subtle form, as when in "Solvejg" he describes gardens on a December evening and succeeds in combining scientific observation with the mood which is always present in his poetry: "where silent gardens slept the dreamless, / peaceful sleep on the bed of fallen leaves, / glad that the bustle of summer was past."

II   Moods (Stemninger, *1892*)

The following volume of poems, *Moods,* shows something of a reaction against the naturalistic observation and pantheism of *Verse.* Here expressing the fear of the forces of nature, Jörgensen anticipates the prose written after his conversion four years later. Thus in "Summer Night Rain" ("Sommernatsregn") he creates an atmosphere of terror reminiscent of Wordsworth's "Peter Bell" * as the raindrops are transformed into thousands of footsteps pursuing the poet, while in the magnificent "Summer" ("Sommer"), with which the volume closes, the same feelings are expressed: "The summer woods are filled with secret sounds, / while the sun casts hot spells in the midday hour, / and the fir-trees' net of branches is gilded with light; / there is a gentle rustling over the bed of leaves— / as though silently, with his finger on his lips, / a god were walking invisible along the brown path . . . / a pang of fear shoots through the bottom of my heart / —is it ancient Pan passing by, / to frighten me from my lair of leaves with his staff?"

There is something strikingly realistic about the sense of fear in these poems, and it can scarcely be seen as a mere flight of fancy. Jörgensen apparently really felt himself threatened by the forces of nature, just as, in the *Legend,* he recounts in all seriousness a visit from Mephistopheles.

Fear is also present in "A Dream" ("En Dröm") with its vision of the day of judgment, though here it is occasioned by pangs of conscience and is thus of a completely different nature. It is in fact not far removed from the ethical awareness that was soon to be seen in the novels *Summer* and *The Tree of Life.* The poet does not directly renounce his past life, but in "To —" ("Til —") he moves a step further away from it and expresses

---

* "The very leaves they follow me—
  So huge hath been my wickedness."

the desire for pure love. In other respects he continues to talk of the dissatisfaction with his life and his feeling of insufficiency which had been present in *Verse*.

Moods is based on the conflict between the life of the poet in Copenhagen and the ideal life represented by his childhood in Svendborg. It is apparent in the prose poem "The Wild Geese" ("Vildgæssene") in which the poet, walking out late one evening, hears the wild geese flying overhead, and they become a symbol of his longing to get away from the present, earthbound life. His urge to escape from his sordid, everyday existence becomes one of the major themes, whether represented by the snow falling in Copenhagen, an image of purity which awakens his longing for Svendborg, or by the picture of children at play, which helps him to return for a moment to a lost paradise.

Stylistically and thematically *Moods* is reminiscent of the novel *Summer*, which comes from the same period. There is the same dualism between night and day, the same sense impressions, the same sporadic use of vaguely religious terminology—soul, eternity—without any direct connection with a Christian attitude. There are the same examples of sound in the distance and of the mysterious power of the moon. All this is found in poems varying from the heavy, regular Byronic strophes of "Summer" to the irregular and complicated lines of "Vignet", with their scattered rhymes and frequent use of enjambement. The language moves from the ethereal and abstract in some of the moonlight pictures to the precise description most obviously exemplified in the prose poem "Frederiksberg Park" ("Frederiksberg Have"): "Deep in the clear water you can see all that insect life unfolding itself which was the delight of your boyhood days. The larvae of the caddis fly crawl with difficulty over the loose, brown bed of mud, dragging with them their houses of snails' shells, tiny mussels, broken twigs and fragments of foliage."

This is a considerable step from the normal ingredients of Romantic poetry, though even this scene is employed in a manner typical of Jörgensen since it leads him to remember his life in Svendborg. The same happens in "Silkeborg", where the lapping of the water is like a *Kuhreigen* calling the exile home. It is amazing how close to the surface memories are in his subconscious.

III   Confession (Bekendelse, *1894*)

Whereas the change in attitude is only just perceptible in *Moods* the next collection of poems, *Confession,* clearly shows the struggle to attain a new and positive view of life which was going on within the poet's mind at this time. It is biographical in concept and covers the entire period from before *Verse* to the publication of the *Book of Travel,* with which several of the poems have a direct connection: the "Chaldea" sonnets were written in La Rocca, and "Confiteor" after Jörgensen's return home. The feelings and moods expressed in this volume are very varied indeed. Two of the poems are themselves given the title of "confession," the first in Danish ("Bekendelse"), closing the first part of the volume and expressing a faith in an eternity, though not a Christian faith, the second bearing the Latin title "Confiteor" with obvious Catholic overtones. According to Emil Frederiksen[1] this poem was added to the collection at the last moment, and thus the volume as a whole came to have a more pronounced Catholic flavor than would otherwise have been the case. The "Chaldea" sonnets which immediately precede "Confiteor"—a confession of sin rather than faith—could be seen as a general statement of Christian rather than specifically Catholic faith.

The early poems in the volume depict the old restlessness and dissatisfaction, and the desire to escape from the grayness of everyday life and its accompanying sense of loneliness and isolation. Gray is the predominant color in these poems—in "Autumn Dream" ("Höstdröm") there is no other color, and the dreariness is increased by the description of the rain and the mist surrounding the poet in his dream, and which he continues to feel when he awakens. The mood of the following poems is the same, and only in "February" ("Februar") is there a sense of movement towards hope, the movement which ends in "Confession." In these poems there is a growing sense of eternity, while "Confession" itself tells of the conflict between two sides of the poet's personality, between his love of things earthly and his longing for things eternal.

After translations of poems by Mallarmé and Stuart Merrill, which in themselves reflect something of Jörgensen's own state of mind, there follows a series of more optimistic, though by no means serene poems in which the poet expresses a longing for peace with himself. Just when he feels he is achieving it, the dramatic intensity of "Evening Melancholy" ("Aftentungsind"), in which grayness and wet dominate the imagery again, indicates renewed hesitation, but the poet turns to God in his misery. Peace returns, and with it an undefinable faith in an eternity.

This faith continues to be expressed in "Spring Gospel" ("Foraarsevangelium"), a group of poems written during a stay in Svendborg in 1894. Although he was there to escape from financial difficulties in Copenhagen, Jörgensen experienced a happy time together with his wife and child in his childhood home, and this happiness is reflected in the poems. They are a tangible expression of the return home which is indicated more symbolically in the novels. Jörgensen is still only at the stage where he has a faith in eternity, but the confidence in a providence, which later played so great a part in both his work and his life, also finds expression here in language strongly reminiscent of some Psalms denoting longing:

"My soul is like a solitary stream, / quietly murmuring and complaining / and, like a flight of birds at night, / following the path of its fate into the distance.

My soul is like a stream running / through dark lands. / There is a reflection of heaven in it, / and one day it will reach the waters of eternity."

In the central section of this cycle the old temptations return, but he renounces them again and finishes with a positive statement of faith in light and the renunciation of night and all it has meant for him. Then come the "Chaldea" sonnets, fifteen of them portraying the poet's considerations as he approaches a positive Christian faith—the thought of renunciation, of sin, of the light of faith. It is the transition from doubt to faith which is depicted in these beautiful and clear philosophical poems, and so it is fitting that the volume should finish with the new "Confiteor," again a piece of lyrical autobiography written from a new standpoint and with new insight. We are now approximately at the same stage as in the *Book of Travel*.

Confession is no longer "eighty pages of melancholy in verse," for there is an upward, dramatic movement resulting from a perfectly consistent development. The poems span ten years and mirror the development of the poet's thought throughout that time. In addition they reflect a considerable development in style, some of the poems being in the style of *Verse* (though without any examples of extravagant ornateness), some belonging to the symbolist middle period, and some showing signs of the simplification which was to become a characteristic of Jörgensen's later work. Through his experiments with rhyme and assonance the poet achieves greater firmness of construction in these than in the earlier volumes, while the "Chaldea" sonnets are a considerable achievement in their own right, with more or less obvious echoes from one sonnet to another.

IV   Poems 1894-98 (Digte 1894-98, *1898*)

Jörgensen's conversion is treated in *Poems 1894-98*, which gives a considerable insight into the entire process. Although his prose works from these years are polemical and filled with apologetic zeal, the poems show him to have been less sure of himself than the prose would indicate, and reveal his inner struggle before his reception and the sense of emptiness he experienced afterwards.

The first half of *Poems* consists of an almost monotonous alternation between a growing attraction to Christianity and a longing back to the life the poet is now leaving. In "A Fresh Meeting" ("Gensyn") he acknowledges the change that has taken place within him, but nonetheless longs for the forest which, in his pantheistic period, he loved so much and where he underwent such profound experiences: "Like a stranger I sit here, / where once I was at home . . . / my green forest, land of my youth, / I cannot forget you."

The group of poems under the title "Italy" ("Vælskland") are all taken from the *Book of Travel* and reflect the variations in mood which that book portrays. The poet's reaction against his first stay in Beuron is mirrored in "Mountain Air" ("Bjærgluft"), where he feels the call of life, while "The Angelus" ("Angelusklokken"), said to have been written the same evening, indicates the same vague religiosity as "Confession." The tension he felt within himself is most obvious in "Anima Anceps":

"There are two voices constantly struggling, / There are two lights of which neither will be extinguished. / There is a desire to plunge into life, / and a longing to suffer with God who is suffering." Nowhere has Jörgensen given a more potent expression to Goethe's "zwei Seelen wohnen, ach, in dieser Brust," to which he often refers.

The appreciation of worldly pleasure is found again in "Love Song" ("Kærlighedens Sang"—a translation of a poem by William Morris), but a more positive attitude to religion returns, even though doubt is still present. Then, in "Golden Mist" ("Gylden Taage"), the most intense poem in the collection after "Anima Anceps," the breakthrough comes. The poet wonders whether his new faith is a result of weakness, whether he is sacrificing worldly enjoyment in vain: "Was I too weak and too little, / Could I not attain the goal? / And so I sat quietly in a peaceful corner? —Am I now sitting condemning / life to the flame and the fire / while its riches stream past / like a never-ending stream?"

These thoughts are seen against the background of a misty autumn scene, but a breeze comes and disperses the mists. And with them the poet's doubts vanish. He resolutely turns his back on the past and concentrates his thoughts on Heaven. After a series of poems in a happier mood, reflecting domestic life, the volume ends with a number of translations of religious poetry, which in themselves indicate that the poet has passed through doubt to a firm conviction.

The drama of this volume finds its expression through a simplified verse form with fewer obvious artistic devices than have previously been found in Jörgensen's work. There is scarcely a superfluous word, hardly a sign of the ornateness of the first poems. The language of symbolism is disappearing and is being replaced by the clarity and simplicity of the poet's mature years.

V Flowers and Fruits (Blomster og Frugter, *1907*)

That the peace of mind Jörgensen appeared to achieve in *Poems* was not to last is apparent from the later prose, and this impression is confirmed by the next volume of poems, *Flowers and Fruits,* which also contains poems written over a number of years and tells of an inner struggle and its resolution. Although the dominant impression of the book is of happiness and confidence, it embraces countless different moods and sensations. There is scarcely a more desperate poem in Jörgensen's entire production than "Qui plasmasti me" in this volume, a short but powerful poem in which he sees his own worthlessness and degradation, and in his despair prays to God that He will redeem him by grace or mercy—he is too small to help himself. Confidence returns in the last poems in the book. Not all of these, however, were from the immediate period concerned: "The Christmas Star" ("Julestjærnen") had appeared in a Christmas publication in 1903, while the beautiful "Prayer" ("Bön") was written as early as 1894, before Jörgensen's conversion. As had been the case with *Confession* and *Poems,* the chronology of the poems is arranged so as to give a concentrated and dramatic expression to the conflict the poet had been experiencing.

Memories from the past are one of the most striking features of *Flowers and Fruits.* "Uncle Jörgen" is remembered in one, Jörgensen's youngest son, Bengt, in another. Happy memories of Svendborg are recalled in "Summer Memories" ("Sommerminder"), while "Old Places" ("Gamle Steder") contains the melancholy inference that the poet is now seen as a stranger in the town of his childhood. There is a profound melancholy about this and some of the other reminiscences; the title poem was written in 1906 when Jörgensen was forty, and the age of forty is one he often referred to with Charles Péguy's comment that forty is a terrible age, when we become what we really are. Thus this volume of poems had a special significance for him.

The "Christmas Star" cycle together with another entitled "Sleep" ("Sövn") forms the center of *Flowers and Fruits.* Each in its own way shows Jörgensen's artistry at its best. "The Christmas Star" encompasses both cosmic vision and intense personal feeling, while "Sleep" reveals his purely technical mastery and the lyrical beauty of his language. In "The Christmas Star" the perspective is constantly narrowed. The poem opens with the thought of the vastness of the universe: "Endless, bottomless, /

without frontier or base . . . / I am struck with terror and over-
whelmed / by this depth of the heavens."

The world is perhaps the only living point in a dead universe,
and the stars are likened to funeral candles. However, as the
constellations change, a new star appears, the Star of Bethlehem: "Among the stars of the night / a clear star stands out /
as no star ever did before / in the sky around the earth."

This star now becomes the focal point of the poem, is given
symbolical dimensions and turned into the lodestar of the poet,
of the pilgrim, a star which is sometimes lost but easily found
again. Finally the poet sees it has led him back to his childhood
faith, and now he can return to the mother to whom he has
brought so much suffering. The figure of the mother can be
understood literally, but it can also be given a symbolical interpretation. The possibility that the mother of the poem should
be equated with the Virgin is emphasized by the traditional use
of stars to represent her—*stella maris* or *stella matutina*.

In "The Christmas Star" the poet's technical mastery is hidden
in the simplicity of the poem and is sensed mainly as a changing,
though never completely restless rhythm. The use of technical
means is much more apparent in "Sleep," where the gentle sleep
of the first section is indicated by the changing, but always falling
rhythm: "Great sleep, gentle mother, / at whose breast we find
rest / as by great silent streams / flowing in peace and darkness."

The transition to a rising, irregular rhythm in the fourth section is sudden and effective after the cradling movement of the
third, and prepares the reader for the completely arhythmical
description of the nightmare: "A pang of anguish, a weight . . .
Woe unto me—am I awake? / I am threatened, hunted. . . .
Someone is following behind me, / I know not who—I know
not the way forward— / I fumble, mistake and shall never find
my way home."

After the nightmare the rhythmical irregularities are gradually smoothed out in the sixth section, finally returning to the
rocking movement of the opening. At the same time the changing
vocabulary in the poem is a clear example of Jörgensen's masterly treatment of the Danish language. In particular, the words
chosen for the most peaceful sections are those which were later
most characteristic of him, and the reader is often surprised

that such a simple choice of words—golden, pure, clear, mild, silent—can lead to such intensity of expression. Again the name of Wordsworth springs to mind as an English parallel: expressions of his such as "And silent is the moon" have much the same quality as Jörgensen's poetry.

VI Out of the Depths (Af det Dybe, 1909)

It is striking how many volumes of Jörgensen's poetry have centered around a personal crisis and shown a progress from doubt to apparent firmness of faith. There is ample evidence to show that this indeed was the case, and thus the next collection, *Out of the Depths*, deals with yet another of them. The title is ambiguous, referring obviously to the *De profundis*, which Jörgensen often quotes: the 129th Psalm in which man prays from the depths for salvation. At the same time there seems to be a reference to the Nordic Agnete myth, in which Agnete marries a merman and goes to live beneath the sea. Throughout this volume there is the thought of being a prisoner of life and youth, together with the longing to break away from these bonds. The poet cannot do it himself, and so prays that God will help him.

Symbolically, the work begins with seven poems from 1885, from Jörgensen's own youth. They are typical of the period, with neologisms and compounds aimed at attaining precision of expression. They are ornate, with obvious examples of onomatopoeia and with artificial metaphor. The symbolism is similar to what we have seen before, with forests shutting out the view, the use of sound in the distance, and the magic of the moonlight. The forests are alive with the old symbols of pantheism, and there is the same fear of the forces of nature as in *Confession*.

In later nature poems the personification has gone, and light replaces the darkness and fear in the early ones. Nature has indeed become a comfort to the poet: "Bright forest from the spring of my life, / who can make me as gentle as a child again / and as quiet and as pure as a child / like the flowers in the grass and the boughs of the beech?"

However, the memories of past times become stronger, and the conflict between youth and life on the one hand and Christianity on the other becomes more obvious. The poet observes that life and time contain no consolation; he sees the vanity of them, though admits that he is still tempted by them, while in the final poem, "The Children Play by the Edge of the Forest" ("Börnene leger ved Skovens Bræm") he returns to the subtle symbolism of earlier poems. From the forest he watches children playing, building houses of sand, and declares that he has done the same thing. The reader senses a wasted youth behind his words, and the burning desire to break with it once and for all. The poet yearns for life, for the heights, but he cannot transform his longing into action, as he admits in "Agnete."

Then comes the thought of death and of the need to renounce the world, though it seems as if Jörgensen is rather trying hard to convince himself than that he has accepted this idea. Nevertheless, in "Good Friday" ("Langfredag") and "The Christmas Rose" ("Julerosen") he humbly hopes that he can obtain faith and be found acceptable despite his weakness.

VII   There Flows a Spring (Der er en Brönd, som rinder, *1920*)

It was eleven years before Jörgensen again published a collection of poems, although a number of his prose works from the period contain some lyric poetry. *There Flows a Spring* is far beyond the period of crises which *Out of the Depths* concluded. Instead we now have poems of memories from Svendborg, and of journeys made to Denmark from Italy, together with poems inspired by the reunification of North Schleswig and Denmark after the plebiscite in 1920. The conflict and tension have gone—some would say this is a loss to the artistic value— and Jörgensen has now progressed to the purity and simplicity which was a feature of all his later poetry. He balances the straightforwardness of his language with a new warmth, a gentle melancholy occasioned by his viewing the past from a distance. The former metaphorical language has almost entirely disappeared, and these poems are practically without metaphor or adornment. Only rarely does a metaphor or an alliterative passage appear, and then, of course, it is used with considerable effect. Although an occasional sound might be heard in the distance, the most striking stylistic devices have been replaced by more subtle techniques; it would be reasonable to talk of an abstraction of nature instead of the fairly precise descriptions of former times. There is a generalized Danishness about the scenery which is almost classical in its lack of individualization: "Here stand the green tree trunks / as in my spring, / and the song of birds rustles / wherever I go. —Sunlight falls between / the distant trees, / and over the bed of leaves / a sheen of bronze. —Fresh air, blue sky, birds / and sun and song. / Alas, everything will begin / once more."

VIII   Aftermath (Efterslæt, *1931*)

Another eleven years had passed before the next volume of poems, *Aftermath,* and while the previous eleven had resulted in the loss of tension as in *There Flows a Spring,* this second period caused a lack of integration between poems. They can certainly be divided into related sections—some religious poems from various periodicals, a number from recent prose works, two elegies, and some new ones with a more personal content: "The Second Hour" ("Den anden time"), "Danish" ("Dansk") and "Departure" ("Afsked"). The new elements comprise a certain preoccupation with modern cultural trends, and also a feeling of advancing age is especially evident in poems such as "The Second Hour," the hour when prayers are said for the dead in Italy; this poem ends with a request that the poet himself should be remembered when his time comes.

Neither are the poems in *Aftermath* unified stylistically. There are no examples of the early ornateness, though some do show a tendency to a rather heavy alliteration which is generally untypical. On occasion, however, it is used with a definite purpose, for instance to stress the wearying effect of a long journey:

> *Træt og tynget, med Stav i Haand,*
> *foruden Værn eller Værge*
> *vandrer den reneste Moder og Mö*
> *over Judæas Bjærge.*

(Tired and weighed down, with a staff in her hand, / without defense or guardian / the purest mother and maiden wanders / over the mountains of Judea.)

IX   Verse from Vadstena
(Vers fra Vadstena, *1941*)

The increased preoccupation with current events which was to
be seen in *Aftermath* makes itself even more obvious in *Verse
from Vadstena,* written in Vadstena during the Second World
War. Whereas the First World War had occasioned a polemical
attack on the Germans, this time Jörgensen was much more
concerned with the general sufferings of humanity, and so the
poems are given the same general significance that Jörgensen
had tended to give his moral observations in the prose works
from this time. The forces keeping the poems together, which
had previously emanated from the poet's inner conflict, are now
external and alien to him. Thus "Good Friday" shows that man's
cries to Christ for help must go unanswered because, as Christ
replies in the last line: "You have crucified both my hands." It
is not the poet who has directed his appeal to Christ, but the
ordinary man with his general doubts—"Lord, *they say* that
you died for us," and it is these people themselves who through
their indifference and skepticism have prevented Christ from
helping them in their need.

Elsewhere there is an idyllic atmosphere to the poems in
Verse from Vadstena, but among these "Fair Isle" ("Fagerö")
deserves special mention, symbolizing Jörgensen's constantly un-
satisfied longing: Fair Isle, the island which cannot be reached,
represents longing backwards in time, longing forwards, longing
from one country to another, to Denmark, to Italy, the longing
the poet feels wherever he is. The last two poems in the volume
were written on his return to Denmark, but the delight in seeing
his native land again is coupled with gratitude for having attained such a great age.

There are nine poems in this volume, and they continue the
process of simplification, which, it must be admitted, is now in
complete harmony with the feelings portrayed. The verse forms
are simple, consisting normally of four short lines, two of which
are usually rhymed. The length of the lines varies somewhat,
while rhymes are sometimes replaced by assonance. Descriptions
of nature are even more abstract than before: "Like a sea the
waves of Vättern / foam towards the shore. / Breaker follows

breaker, / as against the shore of Denmark. —Through the trees on the shore / the autumn wind blows / and I look at the weather vane on the steeple: / the wind is in the southwest."

X   Poems in Denmark (Digte i Danmark, 1943)

Poems in Denmark, published immediately after *St. Bridget,* is much like *Verse from Vadstena,* as the parallel title suggests, and consists of simple poems reflecting momentary moods, nature descriptions, and war poems. "Now the Great Darkness Has Come" ("Nu er det store Mörke kommet") echoes the apocalyptic notes of much of Jörgensen's minor prose from the 1930s, while the three final poems are new examples of the shock technique which he had employed in "Good Friday," when the point of the whole poem emerges suddenly and unexpectedly in the final line. Most striking of these three poems is "Radio," which employs a refrain much on the principle of the refrain in the medieval ballads. It creates the mood of each verse, a threatening undertone in parenthesis, but in the final verse it emerges as the climax: "There towered a church, there stood a house, / Now there lies but a heap of rubble / (destroyed, destroyed). —And sunk at the bottom of the sea / rots food for many a hungry mouth / (destroyed, destroyed). —A mother prays to God for her boy, / then a radio bulletin announces: / Destroyed, destroyed!"

Together with these echoes of the war, there are quiet poems reflecting a gentle happiness such as "Five Years After" ("Fem Aar efter"), written to his wife on their fifth wedding anniversary, and occasional nature poems, of which "Our Sister Snow" ("Vor Söster Sne") stands out as one of the most beautiful poems about snow in Danish. Inspired by St. Francis' "Sun Song," this is a poem thanking God for snow, and at the same time a description of Grib Forest, where Jörgensen lived during the winter of 1942: "Praise be to God for our sister snow— / she is white and pure and exceeding quiet. / She lays her cooling hand over the hot mouth of day, / so all speech must cease. —Praise be to God for our sister snow / she covers the meadows with a cloth under which / the bread can grow; / she gives the young firs a white mantle, so / the frost cannot harm them."

As the themes are simple, so is the construction. The verse forms are predominantly straightforward quatrains with alternating lines, "Our Sister Snow" being the outstanding exception to this.

XI   Ten Poems (Ti Digte, 1946)

Apart from the first poem, a memorial to Harald Thorngren, these *Ten Poems* are sheer descriptions of mood, mostly inspired by events in Vadstena, when both Jörgensen and his wife were ill in the same hospital. The poet is able to make even the most trivial happenings in hospital life poetic—the sound of his wife's shoes creaking along the corridor, a heart she had drawn on a bottle of heart medicine, the shadow of a cross thrown by the window frame. It is a time of sickness and worry, yet the poems are happy in mood, reflecting an inner peace which has become more and more apparent in the poems written since Jörgensen's return to Scandinavia. The inner conflict has gone, and the poet is at peace with himself.

XII   Fyen and Other Poems (Fyen og andre Digte, 1948)

He published one more volume of poems before his death: *Fyen and Other Poems,* but, as he indicates in the foreword, it is a fairly slender volume in content as well as in bulk. There are momentary moods and occasional poems, all recognizably by Jörgensen, but not forming any particular unity. Nor are they all late poems, and so the simplicity of Jörgensen's late style alternates with the compound adjectives of an earlier age, while a poem written on the occasion of the poet's wedding anniversary in 1948 is found side by side with "Christmas Morning" ("Julemorgen"), in which the Christmas bells are sufficient to quiet the noise of the town and bring "peace to each mind torn by conflict." An echo of the distant past.

Jörgensen's lyric poetry thus forms a commentary to his other works as well as to his life. It varies greatly in style from the baroque ornateness of the first volume to the ethereal beauty of the production from the 1940s. It is a progression which is obviously closely allied to his own mental development from the radical, scientific reformer and revolutionary to the pious

Catholic of his later days. His poetry is, after 1896, Catholic in spirit, but his religion is on the whole expressed in general terms and does not result in many emphatically Catholic poems such as those of, for instance, Francis Thompson—whom, indeed, Jörgensen greatly esteemed. Jörgensen's most powerful lyric poems are those expressing the strongest personal emotions, feelings which came as much from himself as from his religion. Thus his best are probably those written between 1894 and 1909, the period of the religious crises, though the later ones should not be underestimated. It is perhaps more difficult to write without a sense of inner conflict, but in these final works Jörgensen set out to express peace of mind—and he succeeded.

CHAPTER 8

Conclusion

IN the nineteen-forties an attempt was made in Sweden, under the leadership of the author and literary critic Harald Schiller, formally to propose Johannes Jörgensen for the Nobel Prize. Jörgensen knew about it, though subsequently both he and his wife said in letters that they had not taken the idea seriously. It was in 1944 that the efforts reached their climax, but that same year the prize went to another Dane, Johannes V. Jensen. There are no signs of real disappointment in Jörgensen's correspondence, but one remark he made on this occasion is almost symbolical of his situation: "The prize was to go to a *typical Dane*—and 'I have brown eyes.'"[1] With this reference to one of his essays in which he uses his brown eyes as a token of his having non-Danish blood in his veins, he sums up his peculiar position, which was to affect both his national and international reputation. He was a Dane, but something of an outsider. Perhaps, in this connection, his thoughts might have gone back to the period at the beginning of the century when, as he relates in his autobiography, he had seriously considered using German as his literary language, but had finally decided that he would continue as he had begun, as a Danish writer.

It was a fateful decision, for on the one hand, by writing in Danish he knew he was going to be forced to rely on translations to make an international reputation, while on the other, he was in opposition to the main trend of thought in Denmark. There he would be bound to encounter prejudice as well as justifiable criticism in the evaluation of the intrinsic quality of his work. To an amazing extent his reputation has surmounted both these difficulties, though in his comment that the Danes fall back on his poetry so as not to consider his real achievement, he reveals his disappointment at the way in which his prose work was received in his own country. It was not without some justification that he called himself "a voice crying in the wilderness."

In Denmark, then, Jörgensen's reputation rests predominantly on his poetry. It has been said, and with some justification, that Jörgensen is today the most popular of the group of poets known as the poets of the nineties, though many literary scholars would probably point to the greater inventiveness and variety of Sophus Claussen. But Claussen is more esoteric than Jörgensen, and has never been among the most widely read and understood of the great poets in a country which is rich in poetry. Jörgensen's work combines great artistry with striking lucidity, and despite his protestations about his not being a typical Dane, his poetry is often very Danish in quality, both in the rhythm of his lines, the homeliness of his vocabulary, and the obvious and deeply felt love of the Danish countryside. Despite Jörgensen's disagreement with the modern Danish outlook, he never lost his affection for the Denmark he had known in his childhood. His poems about the countryside have a timeless quality; those centered on Svendborg bring to life a quality which has only partly passed, and which many look back on with something of Jörgensen's own melancholy.

It should be remembered that Denmark is a country with an easily accessible countryside, in which most families have only to go back one generation to find roots in the rural areas. The landscape makes an immediate impact on them, and has done so ever since the Romantic era at the beginning of the nineteenth century. Almost without exception the poets of the nineteenth century have extolled the beauties of the Danish countryside. Thus Jörgensen is in many ways well within the traditions of Danish literature. The simplicity which he achieves in his later work is likewise a peculiarly Danish quality; foreign readers are often surprised at the apparent simplicity of Danish poetry.

Neither the autobiography nor the book on St. Francis has gained in Denmark anything like the popularity that the poems enjoy, but the *Legend* appeared in a second edition in 1949, while *St. Francis* has been printed in no less than five editions, the latest coming in 1956. Despite the fact that there are numerous biographies and autobiographies written in Danish, it is somewhat difficult to explain the general approval of these as distinct from other works. Perhaps it is because of the obvious warmth and affection with which both are written. The autobiography is a fearless and unhesitating piece of autobiographical introspection which has obviously appealed to a country where literature often has an introspective quality when judged by English and American standards. The success of St. *Francis* was probably due at least in part to the personal attractiveness of this saint, who has exerted an influence far beyond the limits of the Catholic Church.

The remainder of Jörgensen's prose lies outside the traditional scope of Danish literature because of its Catholic content. Even if, as has been demonstrated, there is much more than propaganda and apologetics in this work, it cannot be denied that it is Catholic to an extent that has been unacceptable to the average educated Danish reader. A Catholic novelist or even essayist might have stood a better chance, as indeed was the case with Sigrid Undset in Norway, but to sit down and read a long biography of a saint does demand an effort of will. The hagiographies have been neglected by literary scholars also, who on the whole have argued that Jörgensen's Catholicism places him outside Danish literature proper, instead of realizing that he deserves recognition for adding something new to Denmark's literary wealth.

It was perhaps the very striving for affinity with his subjects which limited Jörgensen's success in Denmark while at the same time providing him with the means to his own particular achievement. He might have had a different reception had he dealt with some of Denmark's own medieval figures, such as St. Ansgar or St. Knud. But Danish saints could evoke no personal response in him, and without that he could not write. More surprising, perhaps, is the fact that he never wrote of Steno, the seventeenth-century Danish anatomist who went to live in Florence and ended his days as a Catholic bishop in northern Germany. Here was a man who could have been expected to appeal to both author and public. However, Jörgensen obviously found no real affinity, and he was an author of sufficient integrity not to tackle a subject merely because he knew it would appeal to his readers.

Outside Denmark, however, it was the strong Catholic content of Jörgensen's work which especially attracted attention to him, and he has achieved universal preeminence among Catholic writers. His book on St. Francis is said to have been translated into more languages than any other Danish work with the exception of Andersen's *Fairy Tales*. This claim may or may not be true, but it is at least indicative of the large numbers of readers this book has enjoyed. In the United States it has also appeared in a paperback edition. None of Jörgensen's other hagiographies has achieved quite the same success, but they have made a marked impact. The book on St. Catherine of Siena was largely responsible for modern research into that saint and is widely considered to be outstanding among the many books which have been written about her.

In Italy and France his name has been widely known for years, and the position is similar in Germany. There, however, he was scarcely spoken of with affection during the years immediately following the First World War, when he had directed a number of polemical attacks on Germany for its treatment of Belgium. In later years, however, the controversy was forgotten, and there, too, he has emerged as a well-known apologist.

Johannes Jörgensen is one of the very few Danish writers who enjoy a worldwide reputation. Andersen and Kierkegaard are outstanding. After them, Danish literary historians might point to the literary influences of Jens Peter Jacobsen and Johannes V. Jensen, but it is probably true that their work is not as widely known as that of Jörgensen. It was not without reason that he was called, in an article appearing in *The American-Scandinavian Review* in 1947, "Denmark's ambassador in world literature—ambassador of world literature in Denmark."

Notes and References

(Editions of Jörgensen's works will be found listed in the bibliography. Where reference in the following is to his *Selected Works, Udvalgte Værker*, I - VII, it is by the abbreviation U.V. followed by the number of the volume.)

Chapter One

1. *Tilskueren*, Oct. 1893, p. 771.
2. Letter to Mogens Kai Nörregaard, 24.III.34.

Chapter Two

1. *Foraarssagn*, p. 62.
2. *Ibid.*, p. 46.
3. Cf. *Legend*, Vol. I, *The Red Star*, pp. 76-77: "It was at this time that my classmates began to go to dancing lessons. *I* did not want to learn to dance. I firmly refused. I thought of physical contact with the girls with the hatred of an ascetic. But there was desire in the asceticism and love in the hatred. . . . Until "she" came—the first love, and all my impure thoughts, all somber, envious hatred burned away in the golden flame."—"She" is, of course, the Anna of *Spring Legend*, and a passage such as this from the autobiography serves as a unique commentary on this first novel.
4. Jörgen Andersen, *Breve fra Johannes Jörgensen til Viggo Stuckenberg* (Copenhagen: Gyldendal, 1946), pp. 51-52.
5. *Foraarssagn*, pp. 65-66.
6. *U.V.* I, p. 71.
7. *Ibid.*, pp. 64-65.
8. *Ibid.*, p. 144.
9. *Ibid.*, p. 165.
10. *Ibid.*, p. 180.
11. *Ibid.*, pp. 130-31. In *Ecce Homo* Nietzsche himself points to this idea as fundamental to *Also Sprach Zarathustra*.
12. J. K. Huysmans, *Against Nature*. Tr. Robert Baldick. (Harmondsworth: Penguin Books, 1959), p. 108.
13. *U.V.* I, pp. 178-79.
14. Letter in Royal Library, Copenhagen.

15. *U.V.* I, p. 212.
16. *Ibid.*, p. 296.
17. *Ibid.*, p. 336.
18. *Foraarssagn*, p. 79.
19. *U.V.* II, p. 443.
20. *Ibid.*, p. 447.
21. *Ibid.*, pp. 458-59.
22. *Ibid.*, p. 9.
23. *Ibid.*, p. 32.
24. *Ibid.*, p. 18.
25. *Helvedfjender (Enemies of Hell)*, p. 79.
26. *U.V.* II, p. 252.
27. *Ibid.*, p. 253.
28. *Ibid.*, p. 127.

Chapter Three

1. Jörgensen had translated some of his work into Danish.
2. *En Apostel (An Apostle)*, pp. 59-60.
3. *Legend*, Vol. 5, *At the Beautiful Temple Door*, p. 29.
4. *U.V.* V, p. 43.
5. *Ibid.*, p. 11.
6. Baudrillart's article is discussed at length in *Legend*, Vol. 5, *At the Beautiful Temple Door*, p. 168.
7. Jörgensen expresses similar feelings in some of his letters to Mogens Kai Nörregaard.
8. *Den hellige Frans af Assisi*, 5th ed., p. 43. The same thought is found in *Legend*, Vol. VII, p. 13: "There are moments in the life of a convert . . . when he feels himself placed between the brilliance of culture and the sufferings of the Savior—when he feels crushed by the mystery of humility and suffering, and when he is gripped by fear: 'Am I right in disdaining the god of earthly advancement and serving the one in Heaven?' " Similarly, in his copy of Robert Hugh Benson's novel *The Necromancers*, which he bought in London in 1913, he has underlined the following passage: "He was, in fact, in that state of religious unreality which occasionally comes upon converts within a year or two of the change of their faith. The impetus of old association is absent, and the force of novelty has died."
9. *Den hellige Frans af Assisi*, p. 12.
10. *Ibid.*, p. 166.
11. *Ibid.*, p. 201.
12. *Ibid.*, pp. 158-59.
13. *U.V.* III, p. 317.
14. *Den hellige Frans af Assisi*, p. 206.

15. *Ibid.*, p. 230.
16. *Ibid.*, p. 216.
17. This had already been published in an old Danish version by C. J. Brandt in his *Dansk Klosterlæsning fra Middelalderen,* 1858.
18. *Den yndigste Rose,* p. 112.
19. *Ibid.*, p. 71.
20. *U.V.* V, p. 92.
21. *Ibid.*, p. 162.
22. *Ibid.*, p. 163.
23. *Ibid.*, p. 196.
24. *Ibid.*, p. 141.
25. *Den hellige Katerina af Siena,* 2nd ed., p. 31.
26. *Ibid.*, p. 83.
27. *Ibid.*, pp. 276-77.
28. *Ibid.*, p. 270.
29. *Ibid.*, p. 14.
30. *Ibid.*, p. 15.
31. *Ibid.*, p. 50.
32. *Ibid.*, p. 270.
33. *Ibid.*, pp. 2-3.
34. *Ibid.*, p. 367.
35. *Ibid.*, p. 26.
36. *Ibid.*, p. 19.
37. Sigrid Undset, *Caterina av Siena* (Oslo: Aschehoug, 1951), p. 31.
38. Blessed Raymond of Capua, *The Life of St. Catherine of Siena.* Tr. George Lamb. (London: Harvill Press, 1960), p. 38.
39. *Den hellige Katerina of Siena,* p. 129.

Chapter Four

1. *U.V.* III, p. 96.
2. *Ibid.*, p. 128.
3. *Ibid.*, p. 215.
4. *Ibid.*, p. 251.
5. *Ibid.*, p. 274.
6. Jörgen Breitenstein, "Johannes Jörgensen og italiensk kultur," *Danske Studier,* 1960, pp. 32-66.
7. *U.V.* III, p. 274.
8. *Ibid.*, p. 327.
9. *Ibid.*, p. 262.
10. *Ibid.*, p. 162.
11. *Ibid.*, p. 187.
12. *Ibid.*, p. 153.

13. *Ibid.,* p. 154.
14. *Ibid.,* p. 194.
15. *Ibid.,* p. 354.
16. *Ibid.,* pp. 402-03.
17. *Ibid.,* p. 358.
18. *Alvernerbjærget,* pp. 81-82.
19. *Ibid.,* pp. 60-61.
20. *Jorsalafærd,* Vol. II, pp. 177-78.
21. *Ibid.,* Vol. I, p. 125.
22. *Ibid.,* Vol. I, p. 126.

Chapter Five

1. Harald Höffding (1843-1931), the philosopher, was a lecturer in philosophy at Copenhagen University when Jörgensen was a student there. He was subsequently appointed professor.
2. *Legend,* Vol. II, *The Tower (Taarnet),* p. 27.
3. *Legend,* Vol. VI, *God's Millstone (Guds Kværn),* pp. 42-43.
4. This is the same Goldschmidt who hounded Sören Kierkegaard in his satirical periodical *Corsaren (The Corsair).*
5. *Legend,* Vol. I, *The Red Star (Den röde Stjærne),* p. 84.
6. The impression this dream made on him is seen not only from the fact that it is described in both the *Legend* and *Our Lady of Denmark,* but also from the number of times Jörgensen mentions it in his diary; in the *Legend* he refers to it in seven entries, spread over sixteen months.
7. *Legend,* Vol. III, *Italy (Vælskland),* p. 54.
8. *Legend,* Vol. IV, *The Unleavened Bread (Det usyrede Bröd),* p. 93.
9. *Legend,* Vol. I, *The Red Star (Den röde Stjærne),* pp. 63-64.
10. *Legend,* Vol. VI, *God's Millstone (Guds Kværn),* pp. 54-55. St. Amandus is another name for Suso.

Chapter Six

1. *Don Bosco,* p. 177.
2. *Ibid.,* p. 179.
3. *Legend,* Vol. VI, *God's Millstone (Guds Kværn),* p. 101.
4. *Don Bosco,* p. 24.
5. *Ibid.,* p. 49.
6. *Ibid.,* p. 197.
7. *Charles de Foucauld,* p. 17. *The Story of a Mother,* one of Andersen's lesser known tales, tells of a mother who, when Death carries away her child, pursues him and reaches his garden, in which

every flower is a child. She seems able to save her son, but finally resigns to the superior wisdom of Death, and allows him to take her child "into the unknown land."

8. *Charles de Foucauld*, p. 109.
9. *Ibid.*, p. 150.
10. *Ibid.*, p. 76.
11. *Ibid.*, p. 125.
12. *Ibid.*, pp. 53-54.
13. *Den hellige Birgitta af Vadstena*, Vol. II, p. 97.
14. *Ibid.*, Vol. II, p. 141.
15. *Ibid.*, Vol. I, p. 16.
16. *Ibid.*, Vol. I, p. 52.
17. *Ibid.*, Vol. II, p. 74.
18. *Ibid.*, Vol. II, p. 210.

Chapter Seven

1. Emil Frederiksen, *Johannes Jörgensens Ungdom*, p. 240.

Chapter Eight

1. Letter to Mogens Kai Nörregaard, 13. XI. 44.

Selected Bibliography

A complete bibliography of works by and on Jörgensen in Danish and other languages until 1950 will be found in: Dahl, Svend & Engelstoft, Povl. (eds.) *Dansk skönlitterært forfatterleksikon 1900-1950,* Copenhagen: Grönholt Pedersens Forlag, 1959-61, Vol. II, pp. 76-87.

Works by Jörgensen Relevant to This Study

Vers. Copenhagen: P. Hauberg, 1887.
Foraarssagn. Copenhagen: P. Hauberg, 1888.
En Fremmed. Copenhagen & Kristiania: P. Cammermeyer, 1890.
Stemninger. Copenhagen: Philipsen, 1892.
Sommer. Copenhagen: Philipsen, 1892.
Livets Træ. Copenhagen: Philipsen, 1893.
Hjemvee. Copenhagen: Philipsen, 1894.
Bekendelse. Copenhagen: Philipsen, 1894.
Rejsebogen. Copenhagen: Ernst Bojesen, 1895.
Den yderste Dag. Copenhagen: Det nordiske Forlag, 1897.
Helvedfjender. Copenhagen: Det nordiske Forlag, 1898.
Digte 1894-98. Copenhagen: Det nordiske Forlag, 1898.
Vor Frue af Danmark. Copenhagen: Det nordiske Forlag, 1900.
Eva. Copenhagen: Det nordiske Forlag, 1901.
Romersk Mosaik. Copenhagen: Det nordiske Forlag, 1901.
Den hellige Ild. Copenhagen: Det nordiske Forlag, 1902.
Romerske Helgenbilleder. Copenhagen: Det nordiske Forlag, 1902.
Pilgrimsbogen. Copenhagen: Det nordiske Forlag, 1903.
Græs. Copenhagen: Gyldendal, 1904.
Blomster og Frugter. Copenhagen: Gyldendal, 1907.
Den hellige Frans af Assisi. Copenhagen: Gyldendal, 1907.
Den yndigste Rose. Copenhagen: Gyldendal, 1907.
Af det Dybe. Copenhagen: Gyldendal, 1909.
Bag alle de blaa Bjærge. Copenhagen: Gyldendal, 1913.
Den hellige Katerina af Siena. Copenhagen: Gyldendal, 1915.
Alvernerbjærget. Copenhagen: Gyldendal, 1920.
Der er en Brönd, som rinder. Copenhagen: Glydendal, 1920.
Jorsalafærd. Copenhagen: Gyldendal, 1923.

Mit Livs Legende. Copenhagen: Gyldendal, 1916-1928.
Vol. I. *The Red Star (Den röde Stjærne),* 1916.
Vol. II. *The Tower (Taarnet),* 1916.
Vol. III. *Italy (Vælskland),* 1917.
Vol. IV. *The Unleavened Bread (Det usyrede Bröd),* 1918.
Vol. V. *At the Beautiful Gate of the Temple (Ved den skönne Tempeldör),* 1918.
Vol. VI. *God's Millstone (Guds Kværn),* 1918.
Vol. VII. *Far off in Italy (Over de valske mile),* 1928.
Second edition, abridged in two volumes, 1949.
Don Bosco. Copenhagen: Gyldendal, 1929.
Efterslæt. Copenhagen: Gyldendal, 1931.
Charles de Foucauld. Copenhagen: Gyldendal, 1934.
Vers fra Vadstena. Copenhagen: Gyldendal, 1941.
Den hellige Birgitta af Vadstena I-II. Copenhagen: Gyldendal, 1941-43.
Digte i Danmark. Copenhagen: Gyldendal, 1943.
Ti Digte. Copenhagen: Gyldendal, 1946.
Fyen og andre Digte. Copenhagen: Gyldendal, 1948.

Jörgensen in English Translation

Pilgrim Walks in Franciscan Italy. Edinburgh & London: Sands & Co., 1908.
St. Francis of Assisi. Transl. T. O'Conor Sloane. New York & London: Longmans, 1908.
Jörgensen: An Autobiography. Transl. Ingeborg Lund. London: Sheed & Ward, 1928-29.
Don Bosco. Transl. Ingeborg Lund. London: Burns, Oates, 1934.
St. Catherine of Siena. Transl. Ingeborg Lund. New York & London: Longmans, 1938.
St. Bridget of Sweden. Transl. Ingeborg Lund. London: Longmans, Green, 1954.

Works on Jörgensen

Andersen, Jörgen. *Breve fra Johannes Jörgensen til Viggo Stuckenberg.* Copenhagen: Gyldendal, 1946.
Frederiksen, Emil. *Johannes Jörgensens Ungdom.* Copenhagen: Gyldendal, 1946.
Jones, W. Glyn. *Johannes Jörgensens modne år.* Copenhagen: Gyldendal, 1963.
Breitenstein, Jörgen. "Johannes Jörgensen og italiensk kultur," *Danske Studier,* 1960, pp. 32-65.

Jones, W. Glyn. "Johannes Jörgensen and his Apologetics," *Scandinavian Studies*, Vol. 32, No. 1, pp. 27-36.

——. "Johannes Jörgensens behandling af visioner," *Catholica* (Copenhagen), Vol. 17, No. 1, pp. 10-20.

——. "Some Personal Aspects of Johannes Jörgensen's Prose Writings," *Modern Language Review*, Vol. LV, No. 3, pp. 399-410.

——. "The Early Novels of Jörgensen," *Scandinavian Studies*, Vol. 36, No. 2, pp. 103-117.

Index

A. Personal names.

Where possible these are referred to by surnames first, but this has not always been practicable, especially for medieval names, and here references are normally in the form to be found in the text.

B. Publications.

Where no other indication is given, the work is by Jörgensen. In all other cases the author's name is given in parentheses after the title, or, where relevant, the fact that the publication is a newspaper or periodical. No reference is made to individual poems by Jörgensen.